MAKING HAND-SEWN BOXES

TECHNIQUES AND PROJECTS

MAKING HAND-SEWN BOXES

TECHNIQUES AND PROJECTS

Jackie Woolsey

Guild of Master Craftsman Publications Ltd

First published 1999 by
Guild of Master Craftsman Publications Ltd,
166 High Street, Lewes,
East Sussex BN7 1XU

© Jackie Woolsey 1999
Reprinted 1999
ISBN 1 86108 085 9

Cover photograph by Zul Mukhida
Photography by Zul Mukhida
Line drawings by John Yates

Designed by Teresa Dearlove
Cover designed by Wheelhouse Design

Typefaces: Caslon and Frutiger

Colour reproduction by Job Color srl – Gorle (BG) – Italy

Printed and bound by Kyodo Printing (Singapore)
under the supervision of
MRM Graphics, Winslow, Buckinghamshire, UK

God grant that I may see to stitch
Until my dying day
And, when the last thread is clipped
And scissors tucked away,
The work that I have done lives on
So other folk may see
The pleasure I have known, Lord,
In the skill you gave to me
Anon.

The author acknowledges, with grateful thanks,
the provision of the fabrics used in the production
of many of the boxes shown in this book by
The Cotton Patch, Specialist Patchwork and
Quilting Company.
(*See* Mail-order suppliers, page 121, for details.)

Contents

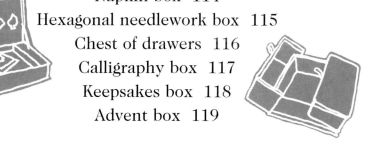

Note on measurements
Throughout the book, both metric and imperial measurements have been given. These are not equivalents but alternatives, and the boxes resulting from the different systems will not be identical in size. For each box, use only one system of measurement.

Introduction

Learning this new hobby could seriously alter your life – making boxes can become addictive! When I first started to make boxes – the result of attending a series of classes organized by my local Women's Institute (WI) – I little dreamt that, many years later, I would still be lacing fabric over card and creating boxes of ever more varied shapes and designs.

Showing others the construction techniques has given me endless pleasure, and in this book I have endeavoured to pass on everything that I have learned through the trial-and-error production of countless boxes.

You will find here all the basic information needed to make fabric-covered boxes, presented in easy stages. There is a degree of logical progression in the arrangement of the projects in this book, but by referring to the Techniques section for anything not yet encountered, you will be able to tackle any of the projects in any order. I would advise you to read through the Techniques and Before You Start sections, before starting any boxes, as consideration must be given to certain features at the design stage.

Once you have acquired the simple skills for making basic fabric-covered boxes, a whole new world may open up, as boxes and their lids provide a perfect medium for

the presentation of other needle techniques: hand and machine embroidery, canvaswork, patchwork, quilting, pulled and drawn thread work, blackwork and goldwork can all be incorporated into the design of a box. A few guidelines for tackling some of these ideas have been included in Simple Lid Embellishments, for those wishing to try them out for the first time.

The construction of handmade fabric-covered boxes is a satisfying skill in itself and there are many different methods and shapes awaiting experimentation and development by the beginner and experienced craftsman alike. The projects outlined in this book are not intended for slavish copying, but as suggestions to inspire. Try experimenting, for example, with various combinations of the glorious fabrics that are available today and notice what a difference this will make to the final product, be it a simple rectangular box or something more complex. After making one or two boxes, you will certainly have your own ideas for others. Looking around as you go about your everyday activities will bring fresh stimulation for imaginative ways to use your newly acquired skills.

Only basic equipment is needed for making the boxes featured in this book and remarkably little fabric is used. The main requirement is time. Making boxes is not a quick activity, as there are several processes to go through at each stage. Cutting the card and fabric, lacing the fabric over the card, joining the pieces together, padding, covering and so on are all quite time-consuming. Boxes are, however, a very satisfying end product and make useful and attractive gifts, so what better way to spend your day or occupy your hands whilst watching television? By cutting everything in advance, I have even laced fabric over card as a passenger in a car!

Good luck and all good wishes for many happy hours of box making.

Jackie Woolsey

WHAT
YOU
NEED

Chapter One
Materials and equipment

A part from the card used in their construction, the materials and equipment used for making boxes can probably all be found around the house, in sewing kits, tool boxes and kitchen drawers. Even fabrics left over from other hobbies may prove suitable for box making, as comparatively little fabric is required.

Fig 1.1 **Materials and equipment for making fabric-covered boxes.**

Essential Materials
The materials listed below are required for all boxes.

Thick card
Thin card
H or HB pencil
Ruler
Set square or protractor
Knife
Metal edge
Cutting surface
Strong thread
Fabric
Basic sewing kit
Curved needle

Thick card

The construction of most padded boxes is based on the use of 2mm ($\frac{3}{32}$in) greyboard (sometimes referred to as strawboard). This is the card used by framers for backing such things as photographs. It is available from craft suppliers and art shops. More often than not, off-cuts will suffice, as the individual pieces required are not large.

The size of the box will dictate the thickness of the card required: a really large box may require a much heavier card. With the exception of the étui, mounting card is not really thick enough for making boxes and is generally too expensive. Having said that, if you happen to have a ready supply of card thinner than 2mm, try using it for smaller boxes or for those where a double layer of card is involved.

Thin card

Card of 1mm (¾₄in) gauge is used as lining for some boxes. It can be cut from cereal packaging, which is just the right weight. (Never throw any thin card away from now on – 'recycle'.) When lacing fabric over card which has pictures and/or lettering on one side, make sure that the face with the printing is uppermost, so that there is no danger of the printing showing through a fine fabric on the finished side.

H or HB pencils

Make sure the pencil has a good, sharp point. This is especially important when measuring out dimensions on card as the thickness of the pencil mark could cause a variation of 1mm (¾₄in) or more. Furthermore, the indentation of a sharp, hard point in the relatively soft surface of the card will make a slight groove, which will help guide the blade of the knife when cutting.

Knife

It cannot be stressed too strongly how vital it is to have a really sharp blade for cutting the card. Since greyboard is quite thick, a utility knife, such as a Stanley knife, with a new blade is ideal for the purpose. Replace the blades frequently as they will blunt quite quickly. There are many and varied types of craft knives on the market: the blades for these are rather more flimsy than the Stanley knife and should be handled with care, using more strokes to cut through the thick card. (If you have access to a guillotine which will cut card, this will prove extremely useful.)

Metal edge

Always use the knife against a metal edge when cutting card. The purchase of a metal safety rule will prove a very worthwhile investment and could save tears and possible bloodshed.

Never attempt to cut card guided by a wooden or plastic ruler. This is dangerous to fingers and will probably ruin the ruler.

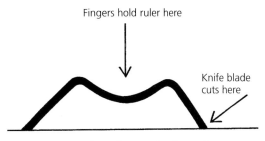

Fingers hold ruler here

Knife blade cuts here

Fig 1.2 **Cross section of a metal safety ruler.**

Ruler

A ruler with well defined markings is essential, as accurate measuring is vital for marking out dimensions.

Set square and/or protractor

It is very important that right angles really are 90° to ensure that the individual pieces of card fit together properly and that the finished boxes are well shaped. For one or two of the box shapes, 45° and 60°/30° angles are called for.

Cutting surface

To protect the surface underneath, place the card on a sufficiently large piece of wood or plastic or, ideally, on one of the cutting mats with 'self-healing' surfaces which have been developed especially for this purpose. For a long-term investment, the A3 size is the most useful.

Strong thread

This is used for lacing fabric over card. Any linen, nylon or polyester thread can be used, or even thin crochet cotton which does not break under tension. The aim is to obtain a smooth, unwrinkled fabric surface when lacing and ordinary sewing threads are not strong enough for this purpose.

Fabrics

There is really no restriction on the types of material that can be used for making boxes. Undoubtedly, fine cottons and polycottons are the easiest to handle and give highly satisfactory results. It is possible, however, to use silks, furnishing fabrics, dupion, corduroy, velvet and thin leathers.

If you are a beginner, I recommend that you use a cotton fabric with a relatively small pattern as the outer covering for your first box, with a co-ordinated plain cotton for the lining. Large patterns require careful planning to ensure that the elements of the design fall in the right places on the box: striped fabrics need particularly careful handling to ensure that the stripes are in correct alignment with the edges of the box.

Always take care to cut with the grain of the fabric and ensure that all pieces are cut from the same warp or weft. The appearance of the colour and texture of fabrics can vary greatly according to how the light falls on them and it is important to take this into account so that the effects are planned rather than a surprise!

Making boxes is an excellent way of using small, leftover lengths of fabrics which have been used for curtains, bed covers, cushions, upholstery, etc.: this will also provide another element of co-ordination in room furnishing.

If you are embellishing your box lid with such things as embroidery, beads or ribbons, the outer fabric for the remaining surfaces will need to be carefully selected so that the decoration and fabric are complementary and so that the fabric is appropriate for the particular embroidery technique. The box sides can also be decorated. All decoration should be carefully planned. A few basic suggestions for decorating boxes are given in Simple Lid Embellishments and there are, of course, many books available on needle techniques which would be suitable for the embellishment of boxes.

Sewing kit

Just a few basic sewing items are required for making hand-sewn boxes:

- sewing threads to match or tone with the chosen fabrics;
- large scissors for cutting out; and
- finer scissors for cutting sewing threads.

Resist the temptation to use scissors for cutting even the thinnest card: this will spoil the blades for cutting fabric and will not give a satisfactory edge on the card.

Needles

The following needles are required to achieve a satisfactory finish:

- a large-eyed, strong needle for the lacing threads;
- smaller, sharp needles for over-sewing the fabric surfaces together and sewing with ordinary threads; and
- a curved needle for ladder stitching the edges of the fabric-covered cards.

For the best results, the curved needle should be as fine as possible and the smallest you can comfortably handle. Through trial and error, I have found that a 'flat, half-round, size 12' (that is, the radius of the curve is 12mm) is the most useful. A curved needle is absolutely essential for achieving a neat finish when making boxes and time spent mastering the technique will bring its own reward.

Additional Materials

The materials listed below are optional extras or required for specific projects in this book.

Padding
Iron-on interfacing
Fray check
Pair of compasses
Compass cutter
Adhesive tape
Double-sided tape
Paper fasteners
Stick glue
Sewing machine
Zip-foot attachment for sewing machine
Sandpaper

Padding

Practically any thin wadding, foam or felt (even strips of blanket) can be used to pad the sides and lids of boxes. The thickness of the padding used depends entirely upon the effect required and, if necessary, more than one layer can be used. However, make these layers one at a time and keep them in the same order when removing and replacing them, as each layer will be slightly larger than the previous one.

Iron-on interfacing

This is particularly useful, applied to the wrong side of the fabric, when preparing mounts as it not only stiffens the fabric slightly but also helps to prevent fraying when cutting into tight corners.

Fray check

I use the words 'fray check' to describe a substance which can be applied to the edges of fine fabrics to prevent fraying as they are cut and handled. There are various products on the market, even one by Newey called 'Fray Check', but PVA glue will also serve the purpose.

Pair of compasses

If you are going to tackle round, hexagonal or octagonal shapes, a pair of compasses is essential. Make sure that the pencil you use has a sharp point and that the compasses can be fixed firmly at the chosen radius without slipping.

Compass cutter

This is similar to a pair of compasses but a cutting blade has been substituted for the pencil. It is not an essential item but it does simplify cutting card circles. The cutting blade should be really sharp.

Adhesive tape

This is used for fastening card faces together. I recommend masking tape. Transparent tapes have a tendency to discolour and become brittle over time and, although adhesive tapes are incorporated into the construction of the box and do not show, it's better to be safe than sorry!

Double-sided tape

This is primarily of use when mounting embroideries and other forms of embellishment which are not applied directly to the surface of the fabric: it is very helpful in holding the worked piece to the frame.

Brass paper fasteners

These are used, pushed through card and fabric, to provide 'feet' on which the boxes can stand. You should exercise some constraint in their use, bearing in mind where the box is likely to be sited, as fasteners may scratch a polished surface.

Paper fasteners with washers

A stronger and bigger but flat version of the fasteners described above, these are used in the two- and three-tier boxes for attaching the trays to the sides of the outer casing.

Glue

The boxes described in this book are made by sewing the fabrics and I would not recommend glue as a substitute. Although new glues, including fabric glues, are being constantly developed, in my experience, these do tend to discolour or lose their grip with the passage of time and, consequently, cannot be regarded as totally reliable. They can also be very messy to use and can so easily be carelessly transferred to areas of fabric where they are not required and ruin hours of work.

However, having said all that, there are one or two places where fabric is not involved and it is card surfaces that are being joined together and, in this situation, a stick glue such as Pritt or Uhu can safely be used. The card pieces should then be left to dry under pressure.

Sewing machine

Whilst not essential, the use of a sewing machine can simplify the task of sewing seams and give a neater, more satisfactory result, particularly for the outer coverings of the padded fabric boxes.

Zip foot attachment for the sewing machine

Again, whilst not essential, this type of sewing machine fitting is particularly useful when sewing seams in the construction of drawers and certain types of lids.

Sandpaper

If the edges of card pieces feel sharp or rough, they can be lightly sandpapered prior to lacing to smooth them off. A fine grade sandpaper is best for this job.

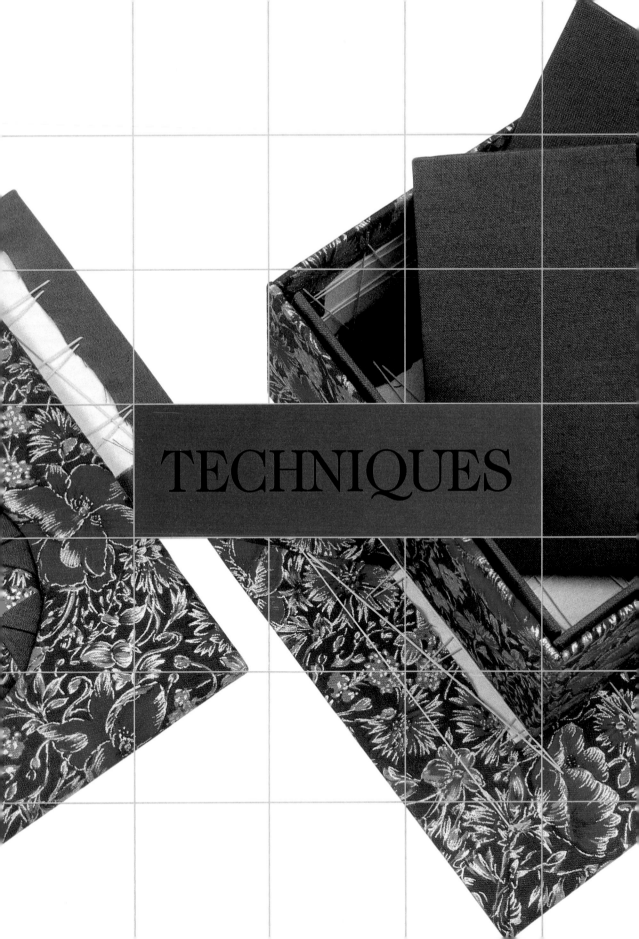

TECHNIQUES

Chapter Two
Basic box making

Time spent accurately marking out and cutting card, using the correct tools, and selecting carefully co-ordinated fabrics will have its reward in the production of a pleasing box.

Marking the card

It is important to rule out the dimensions of the box you are going to make and mark them accurately with a sharp pencil. For a few boxes all the card can be cut out at the beginning but with most projects, the card for the box carcass (the base plus the sides) is cut first and the dimensions for the other card pieces are calculated later, when the first pieces have been covered and joined. The type of card used and the thickness of the fabric covering both have a bearing on these measurements.

Ensure that all the corners are right angles by using a set square or protractor to check each one. Always double-check the dimensions carefully before starting to cut the card pieces.

Cutting the card

It is extremely important that the card is cut accurately – a mistake in the early stages of making a box cannot be corrected later! Working on a special cutting surface,

cut the card carefully along the pencil lines, using a strong utility knife, such as a Stanley knife, held against a metal edge. Position the metal edge on the pencil line and, holding the knife against it, draw the blade steadily towards you with a firm but gentle pressure. Repeat the stroke until the card is cut through. The indentation made by the sharp pencil provides a groove which helps to keep the knife in position on the first stroke and thereafter, the blade will follow the previous cut if a constant, steady pressure is maintained.

Do not try to cut through the card in one stroke and do not use a lot of pressure – pressing really hard can cause wobble! It is far better to use steady, gentle pressure and repeat the action as many times as required: with a sharp blade, this will seldom be more than three.

As each piece of card is marked out, write the dimensions on it in pencil. It is so easy to become confused when several pieces of card are being cut out at the same time, especially if they are similar in size or there are several people cutting together.

Chamfering

Where a very precise corner fit is important, for example, when making risers or trays, or for the triangular box described in Chapter 17, it can be advantageous to chamfer the edges of the card pieces to make them fit together at the corners very closely. This is achieved by holding the knife at the appropriate angle and cutting along the edge of the card. Mark and cut the card to the required finished dimension and then chamfer as indicated in Fig 2.1.

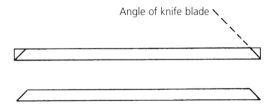

Angle of knife blade

Fig 2.1 **Chamfering card.**

Lacing fabric over card

This is a method of covering card with fabric by sewing. Cut the fabric to be laced not less than 15–20mm (½–¾in) larger all round than the card to be covered; the fabric will measure 30–40mm (1¼–1¾in) more than the card in each direction.

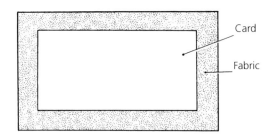

Card

Fabric

Fig 2.2 **Lay the card on the wrong side of the fabric, along the straight grain.**

Lay the card on the wrong side of the fabric, on the straight grain, fold the fabric tightly over the card along two opposite edges, and pin securely. Always position the pins with their heads pointing inwards, as indicated in Fig 2.3. This avoids the fabric riding up the pin when the thread is tightened to tension it.

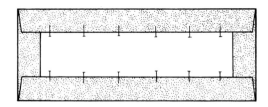

Fig 2.3 **Fold the fabric along two opposite edges of the card and pin securely.**

Always use strong thread for lacing (*see* Chapter 1, page 6). This will enable you to tension the fabric without the thread snapping and will help you achieve a wrinkle-free surface.

It is important to allow the needle to 'take a bite' from the fabric, as shown in Fig 2.4, rather than just passing it through the fabric, which could lead to a fine fabric fraying as the lacing thread is tensioned. Use a large-

Fig 2.4 **Lace the fabric over the card, with the needle always pointing in.**

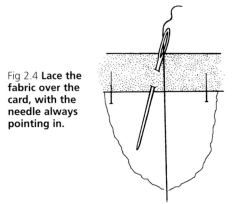

eyed needle and work each stitch with the needle pointing inwards (*see* Fig 2.4).

By threading the needle and, rather than cutting off a length, leaving the thread attached to the reel until the lacing stitches have been taken the length of the fabric, it is possible to tension the lacing by working backwards and gradually tightening the lacing, holding it at each stitch point. When the first stitch is reached, knot the thread off. This avoids waste or having to join on a new length of thread.

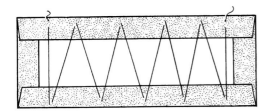

Fig 2.5 **Finish lacing one pair of sides and secure them before lacing the second pair.**

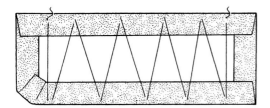

Fig 2.6 **Pull the first corner down, tucking one edge under.**

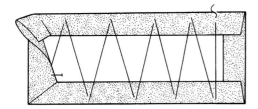

Fig 2.7 **Pin this corner securely.**

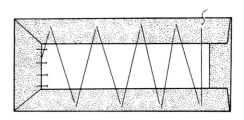

Fig 2.8 **Repeat the process for the second corner, then pin along the length of that side.**

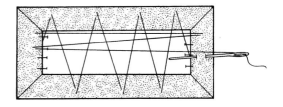

Fig 2.9 **Follow the same procedure for the opposite side before lacing the two sides together.**

Following the sequence shown in Figs 2.5–2.9, lace one pair of opposite sides and fasten off the thread, fold the fabric over the card for the other pair of sides, mitre the corners carefully, and lace as before.

Try to ensure that the mitred surface occurs on the edge which will be the surface on view after the box is finished.

If using a pale or transparent fabric through which the greyboard is likely to show, cut white paper to cover the board and position this prior to lacing.

Ladder stitch

This stitch is used to join two fabrics or fabric-covered cards invisibly. Bring the needle up in one fabric then take it down in the second fabric, in line with the first stitch. This stitch between the two fabrics should be at right angles to the seam. Bring the needle up in the second fabric, a short distance from the previous stitch, then take it down in the first fabric as before. Continue with this process along the length of the seam. When the seam is tightened, the stitches should be almost invisible.

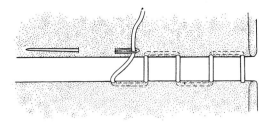

Fig 2.10 **Working ladder stitch.**

Using a curved needle

The efficient use of a curved needle enables two flat, fabric-covered surfaces to be joined together invisibly with greater ease. Ladder stitch is employed as above but the curved needle makes this a simpler operation.

Fig 2.11 **The curved needle in use.**

Stitching side pieces to base card

Place one fabric-covered side card on one edge of the covered base, covered face to covered face, and sew the edges together through the fabric, as shown in Fig 2.12. (A simple oversewing stitch is sufficient.)

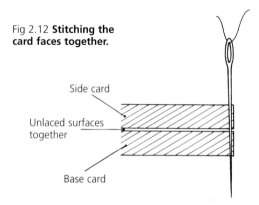

Fig 2.12 **Stitching the card faces together.**

Side card

Unlaced surfaces together

Base card

Joining the corners of the box carcass

When stitching the side pieces to the base to form the box carcass, it is important to give added strength to these corners. Do this by starting to stitch about 20mm (¾in) below the top, taking the stitches up to the top and then working down to the bottom and up again for another 20mm (¾in) before finishing off.

Padding

Padding can consist of any soft material. There is a variety of waddings available for the purpose and felt can be used to advantage in achieving a more tailored finish where a thin layer is more sympathetic than no padding at all.

Individual pieces of card can be covered with padding material, prior to lacing with fabric, to give a raised or shaped surface (usually to the lid), or a whole box can be encased with padding before fitting a complete outer cover. The number of layers required depends on the effect desired.

When fitting a layer of padding around a box, do not overlap the padding edges but cut them so that they butt together, and stitch them as shown in Fig 2.13 so that the final surface is smooth.

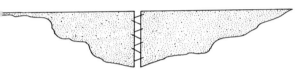

Fig 2.13 Above and below:
Stitching the butted edges together.

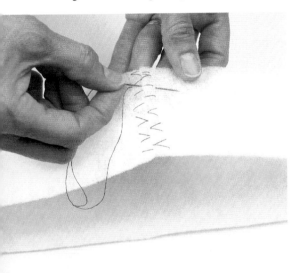

Fig 2.14 **The zip foot positioned against the fabric-covered card.**

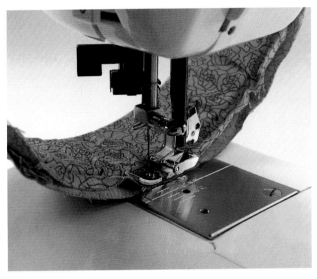

Using the zip foot

When the card has to be completely encased in fabric without the use of lacing, as is necessary in the construction of some lids and drawers, the zip foot attachment on a sewing machine can be extremely useful in making a neat, tight seam.

Pin the fabric tightly over the card, line the zip foot up against the card (*see* Fig 2.14) and keep it in this position as you sew.

Chapter Three
Lids

Fig 3.1 **Lids can be made with or without lips, flush, overlapping or drop-in.**

A great variety of lid styles are available for boxes. The decision about which one to choose should be made at the design stage, since the type chosen will influence the height of the box lining.

Lids Without Lips

To avoid having to fiddle to open a lid without a lip, a ribbon or tab can be fitted between the lid and its lining so that it will protrude slightly and provide a means of opening the lid without having to touch the fabric (see Fig 3.2). This is especially useful if a delicate material has been used.

Fig 3.2 **For a tab, a section of folded ribbon is fitted between the outer lid and the lining.**

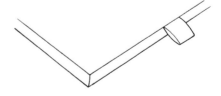

Overlapping flat lid

This is a very uncomplicated lid to construct. It consists simply of a piece of thick card cut to the required dimension, slightly larger than the carcass of the box, padded if appropriate and laced with the chosen fabric. A smaller piece of card is sewn to the underside of the lid, to hold it in place on the box.

Fig 3.3 **Overlapping lid.**

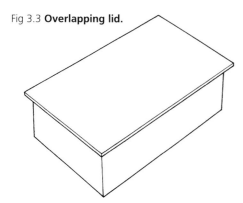

To construct this smaller piece, measure the internal dimensions of the box and cut a piece of thin card such that, when it is laced with lining fabric, it will just fit inside the box when the lid is in position. Attach the lining card to the laced surface of the lid using ladder stitch with a curved needle.

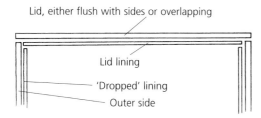

Lid, either flush with sides or overlapping

Lid lining

'Dropped' lining

Outer side

Fig 3.4 **Section through box showing card arrangement for pop-on, overlapping lid.**

Overlapping, flat, hinged lid

The same card dimensions are used as for the unhinged lid, but a hinge is incorporated into the box carcass as it is being constructed. For padded boxes, having joined the base lining and sides together, the hinge is positioned prior to attaching the outer cover. (For full instructions, *see* Chapter 9, pages 40–1.) For double-layer boxes (*see* pages 70–97), position the hinge between the outer sides and the lining pieces before stitching these together.

A hinge is attached to the lid in the same way for both padded and double-layer boxes. (*See* Attaching the lid to the box in Chapter 9, page 44.)

To give a good finish to a hinged lid and prevent it from falling backwards, fix a stay or stays to hold the lid open at a chosen angle (*see* Chapter 4).

Flush flat lid

This lid sits on the top of a box, its edges exactly flush with the sides, so it definitely requires a method of opening (either a tab on the edge or a pull on the top) to avoid over-handling in use. Measure the top

Fig 3.5 **Flush lid.**

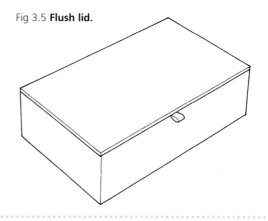

dimensions of the finished carcass and cut a section of thick card following these, allowing for the card to be covered with fabric. It is important to make sure that the finished lid really is flush for a good effect. To hold the lid firmly in place, the lining fits inside the box.

Drop-in lid

This style of lid can be fitted to a tailored box, which has its inner sides at a lower level than the outer sides of the box on which the lid rests. Take the measurement for this lid across the inside of the box carcass and cut a piece to fit from thick card. Decorate, pad and lace as required (*see* Chapter 2). Cut the lining for the lid from thin card so that this, when covered with fabric, will sit inside the lining of the box. (*See* Figs 3.6 and 3.7.)

Fig 3.7 **Section through box showing card arrangement for box with drop-in lid.**

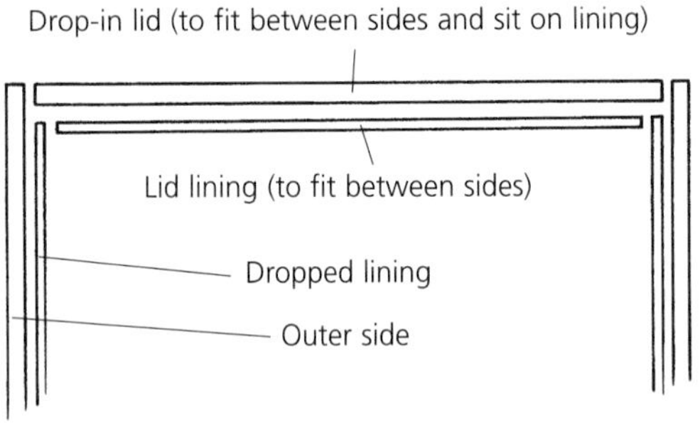

Drop-in lid (to fit between sides and sit on lining)

Lid lining (to fit between sides)

Dropped lining

Outer side

Lids With Lips

Since the lip of the lid will be the means of removing the lid from the box and will, therefore, be handled frequently, consideration should be given to the fabric used to cover it. If the lid is heavily decorated or in a particularly fine or delicate fabric, then the lip is a useful device as it avoids wear on the fabric of the lid itself.

Overlapping lid with lip

Consider the depth of the lip in the design stage and keep this in proportion to the finished box. Do not allow the lip to cover more than one-third of the sides of the box.

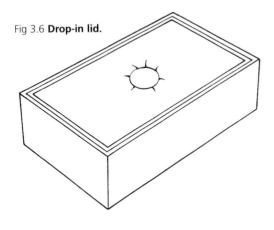

Fig 3.6 **Drop-in lid.**

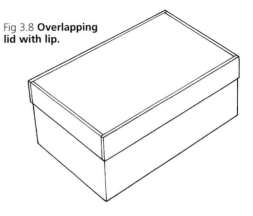

Fig 3.8 **Overlapping lid with lip.**

If you want the lid to enclose the carcass completely, the box itself will need to be mounted on a platform base so that the lid can be more easily removed, without having to turn the box upside down to do so.

Fig 3.9 **Box with full overlapping lid and platform base.**

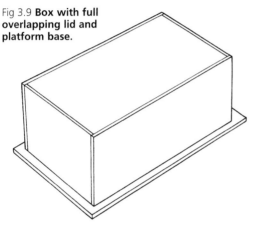

The lid can either sit on the lip, in which case the top of the lid will be unbroken, or be framed by the lip. In this case, the lip can provide an enhancing frame for the lid fabric or any embellishment that has been worked. (*See* Figs 3.10 and 3.11.)

Fig 3.10 **Section through box showing card arrangement for lid with under lip over rising lining.**

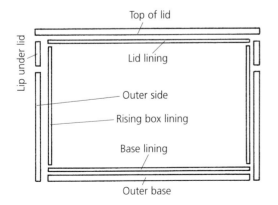

Lip under lid

Top of lid

Lid lining

Outer side

Rising box lining

Base lining

Outer base

Fig 3.11 **Section through box showing card arrangement for lid with framing lip over rising lining.**

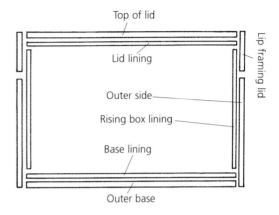

Top of lid

Lid lining

Outer side

Rising box lining

Base lining

Outer base

Lip framing lid

Lid with lip flush with box sides

The lip of a lid can be made so that it lies flush with the sides of the box. This involves making a rising lining for the box at the construction stage, which can only be done using the double-layer method.

Fig 3.12 **Box with flush lid on rising lining.**

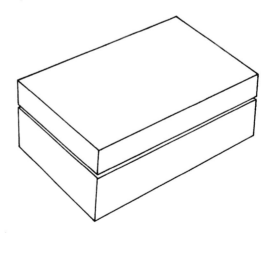

19

Covering the lip of a lid

The lip of the lid should be covered using the same method as the carcass, in accordance either with the padded or the double-layer method. (*See* Chapter 2, pages 12–13.) Take careful measurements according to the type of lip and lid chosen, and allowing for the fabric covering as usual.

In the case of round and oval boxes, and boxes with curved ends, the lip for a flush lid on a rising lining should be cut and moulded at the same time as the base. For an overlapping lip, put the finished carcass in a polythene bag and exclude the air. I do this by inserting a straw in the neck of the bag and sucking it out. This does not, of course, form a vacuum, but it does extract sufficient air to cause the polythene to cling tightly to the carcass and form a water-tight skin. Secure the bag with a tie or elastic band. Mould the card for the lip around

this, first dampening it by stroking it on both sides with a moist sponge. This makes it pliable enough to bend easily around the carcass. Leave the card to dry overnight before removing it, then pad and cover it as described in Chapter 2 on page 14.

You will need to pull round the seam in the fabric that is covering the lip to allow the lid to sit correctly.

Fig 3.13 **Seam pulled round at right angles to allow lid to sit inside lip.**

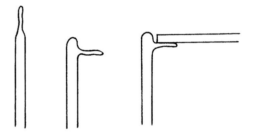

Chapter Four
Lid stays

Fig 4.1 **Stays hold a lid open and steady.**

Stays, which can be made from ribbons, braid or strips of fabric, are positioned between a hinged lid and the box carcass in order to hold the lid open at a consistent angle. (*See* Fig 4.1.) Use a ribbon or braid which is not too stiff so that it will 'fall' naturally into the box as the lid closes.

The stays should be placed in position after constructing the carcass of the box and prior to adding any dividers or stitching the outer covering in place.

Positioning

To establish the position of the ribbon on the outside of the carcass, use a 45° set square and line up the ribbon against it. Leave enough ribbon at one end to overlap the outside of the carcass by approximately 25mm (1in) and leave enough lying inside the box to reach to the lid and allow for stitching into place underneath the lid lining.

One stay may be sufficient but, if using two, measure carefully to ensure that the

Fig 4.2 **Finding the appropriate position for the stays.**

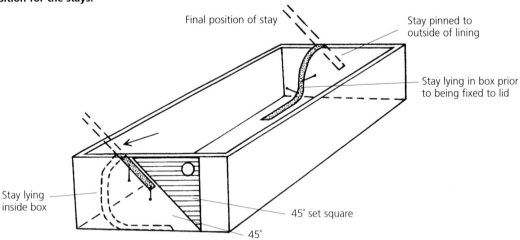

Final position of stay

Stay pinned to outside of lining

Stay lying in box prior to being fixed to lid

Stay lying inside box

45° set square

45°

second stay is at the same angle and in the same position as the first.

Securing

Pin the ribbon over the side of the carcass so that it is out of the way. This end of the stay will be stitched into place when the outer covering fabric is being attached. The other end of the stay is stitched into position when the lid is hinged.

After pinning the lid and the lining into position, push the end of the ribbon between them and pin it firmly in place. If you are using two stays, check that the length of each is the same and that the lid will be held at the correct angle when the stays are holding it. Make sure that the stays are caught in place as the lid and lining are being stitched together, using the curved needle.

Chapter Five
Dividers

Fig 5.1 **Dividers enable the contents of a box to be kept separate.**

Dividers are placed in a box to enable its contents to be kept in separate sections. They can be variously arranged according to requirements.

Dividers should be fixed in position once the carcass has been constructed, prior to padding and covering.

Measuring and positioning

Decide what purpose the divider or dividers are to serve and establish the best positions for that purpose. If there is also to be a tray, involving risers for support (see Fig 6.1), any dividers should be the same height as or slightly lower than the risers.

Measure the internal dimensions of the carcass where the divider is to be positioned. The height of the divider should be rather less than the height of the carcass in order to allow for the lid lining when the lid is closed. Allowance for the thickness of the covering fabric should also be made in determining the other dimensions of the divider.

Fig 5.2 **Alternative positions for a divider in a rectangular box.**

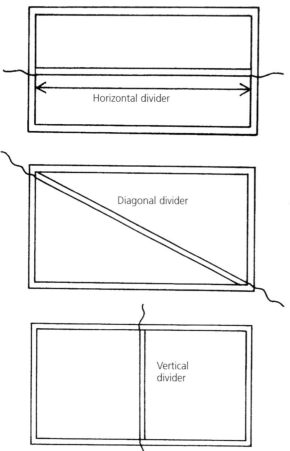

Cutting and covering

Draw the dimensions of the divider on thick card (or on two pieces of thin card), and cut out.

Next, cut out sufficient fabric to cover the divider. For thick card, you will need twice the depth of the card plus turnings, as only the one piece of card is used so the fabric must cover both sides. Before folding the fabric down and stitching, lay two or three pieces of strong thread along the length of the divider, with several inches protruding on either side as shown in Fig 5.3.

Fig 5.3 **Covering a divider made from thick card with fabric.**

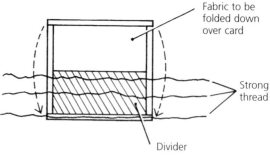

If using thin card for the dividers, two pieces of card are required. Cut fabric for these and lace in the usual way. Lay two or three pieces of strong thread along the length of one piece of card, on the laced surface, then join the two pieces of card neatly, laced surfaces together, by oversewing along the edges with a matching sewing thread. (*See* Fig 5.4.)

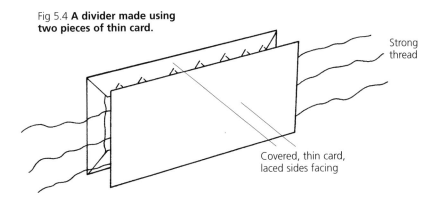

Fig 5.4 **A divider made using two pieces of thin card.**

Strong thread

Covered, thin card, laced sides facing

Securing

Fix the divider in position by using a strong needle to pass each protruding thread either:

- through the joins in the box carcass at the required points; or
- through the sides of the carcass (mark the relevant points and pierce the card first).

For each method, tie off the threads firmly. They will be concealed when the carcass is covered. (*See* Fig 5.5.)

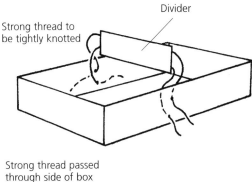

Divider

Strong thread to be tightly knotted

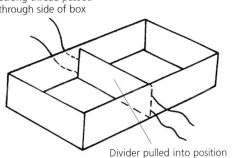

Strong thread passed through side of box

Divider pulled into position

Fig 5.5 **Fixing the divider in place.**

Ring supports

It is possible to include dividers in a jewellery box to act as ring supports. Cut out two dividers in thick card to the required dimensions. Pad one face of each divider (*see* Chapter 2, page 14) and cover with fabric as previously described, lacing over the padded surface (*see* Chapter 2, page 12). Join the dividers at the ends, padded faces together, prior to insertion. This provides a space into which rings can be pushed. Ring supports must be made sufficiently low to allow the lid to close comfortably when rings are in place. (*See* Fig 5.6.)

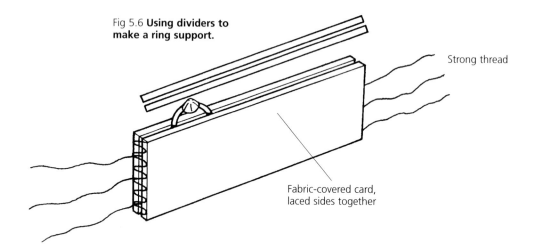

Fig 5.6 **Using dividers to make a ring support.**

Strong thread

Fabric-covered card, laced sides together

Chapter Six
Risers

Fig 6.1 **Risers provide the support for any trays that are fitted in a box.**

Risers are pieces of covered card which, stitched to the sides of a box, provide support for any trays incorporated into the design. (*See* Fig 6.1.)

If a tray or trays are to be provided, it is essential to cut the risers for the tray support at the same time as cutting the sides of the box and to sew them into position after attaching the sides to the base and *before* joining the sides together at the corners of the box.

Measuring and positioning

Having established the size and shape of the box, decide on the depth of the tray in comparison with the height of the box carcass. Do you want it to occupy half of the box or a smaller proportion? The depth of the tray will determine the height of the risers. Bear in mind that the lid lining, if that is to be padded, will take up space inside the box. The height of the tray and the riser should allow for this.

If there are to be divisions in the box as well, then they must be of such a height that they enable a tray to be removed and replaced easily.

Cutting and covering

There are two alternative methods for making risers.

One way is to make them the same length as the sides of the box to which they are to be attached and to chamfer the ends (*see* Chapter 2, page 11) so that they abut neatly to the adjacent risers.

The alternative is to cut each riser shorter than the side to which it is to be attached by twice the thickness of the card; for example, if the card is 2mm (³⁄₃₂in) thick, the riser will be 4mm (³⁄₁₆in) shorter than the side of the box.

Lace the lining fabric over the risers in the usual way (*see* Chapter 2, page 12). If you have used the chamfering method to cut the card, place the lacing on the unchamfered surface.

Attach the sides of the box to the base, then sew each riser to its appropriate side piece, laced surface of riser to unlaced surface of side, making sure that the bottom edges are level. Attach the riser along the bottom and side edges, using ladder stitch with a curved needle. (*See* Fig 6.2.)

Once all the risers are in position, join the sides of the box together at the corners by oversewing in the normal way.

Edges of riser to be stitched into position (top edge left unstitched)

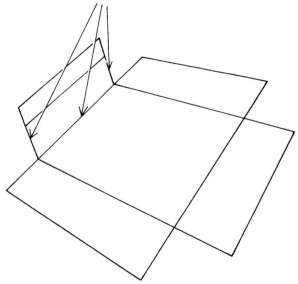

Fig 6.2 **The riser is stitched along three sides, using a curved needle.**

Chapter Seven
Trays

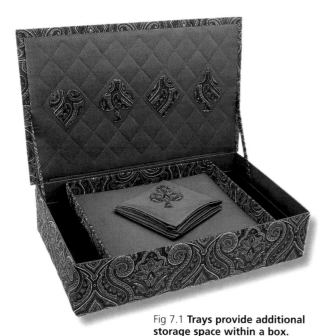

Fig 7.1 **Trays provide additional storage space within a box.**

Trays are an excellent way of providing additional, versatile storage space within a box, enabling a second layer to be included. In a rectangular or square box, the tray can slide on the risers so that access to the lower section can be obtained. (See Fig 7.1.)

While it is important that risers are fitted at an early stage – when the lining pieces are being made – once they are in place, the tray can be constructed at any time, even as the last item, since it is not actually fixed into position in the box.

Rectangular Tray

Measuring and cutting the sides

For the side pieces of the tray, measure across the appropriate part of the box and cut two pieces of card using this dimension as the length of the card and the required height of the tray for the width.

Place these cards carefully in position, measure the distance between them and cut two more pieces of card using this measurement for the length and the required height of the tray for the width.

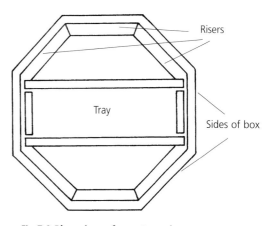

Fig 7.2 **Plan view of a rectangular tray in an octagonal box.**

Risers

Tray

Sides of box

29

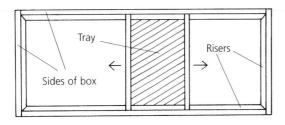

Fig 7.3 **A tray can be made to slide along risers, giving greater access to the layer underneath.**

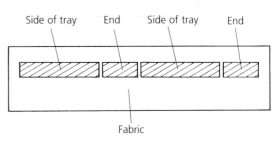

Fig 7.4 **The card sides positioned on the fabric.**

Covering the sides

Lay these pieces of card in a line on the wrong side of the chosen fabric, flat and in the correct order (one long, one short, one long, one short). Cut a piece of this fabric twice the width of the card plus seam allowance (*see* Fig 7.4).

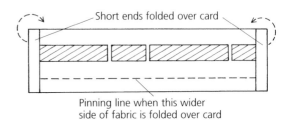

Fig 7.5 **Folding the short ends over the card prior to folding over the long side.**

Fold the short ends of the fabric over the end cards, then fold the wider side of the fabric over the card pieces and pin it tightly against the cards on the other side. (The dotted line shown in Fig 7.5 should now be the line along which the fabric is pinned.)

Either by hand or using the zip foot on a sewing machine (*see* Chapter 2, page 15), sew along the long edge, close to the edge of the card.

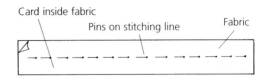

Fig 7.6 **The fabric pinned along the card pieces, ready for stitching.**

Slide the seam around the card in such a way as to manoeuvre it sufficiently far up to allow for a piece of covered card to lie flush within the sides of the tray.

Stitch across the ends of the fabric once the seam has been moved.

Form the four pieces of card into a rectangle, with the seam on the inside, and ladder stitch the two ends together using a curved needle. Make sure that the pieces of card lie correctly, as indicated in the rectangular tray shown in Fig 7.2.

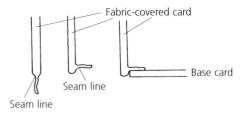

Fig 7.7 **The seam pulled around to allow for the covered card to be positioned within the sides.**

Measuring and covering the base

Measure the internal dimensions of the tray and from these cut a piece of thick card for the base of the tray.

Lace a piece of fabric over this card in the usual way (*see* Chapter 2, page 12) and introduce it into the underside of the tray, beneath the seam, with the laced surface uppermost. Ladder stitch the base into position on the underside, using a curved needle.

Cut a piece of lightweight card to the same dimensions as this base, and lace with fabric. Place this covered card inside the tray, laced side down, to form the lining of the tray. Use glue to stick the two card surfaces firmly together and leave to dry under pressure.

Hexagonal Half Tray

Measuring and cutting the sides

Measure across the diagonal of the box. Cut a piece of card for one side of the tray, using this measurement as the length and the depth of the required tray as the width.

Three smaller pieces of card will be needed for the other sides of the tray. Find the inner measure of one side of the box and use this measurement for the length of each piece and the required depth of the tray for the width.

Covering the sides

Number the tray side pieces and lay them in the correct order on a piece of fabric. While in this instance the three smaller sides have the same dimensions, and the order would

thus be immaterial, numbering all pieces of card used in the construction of drawers and trays is a good habit to cultivate. Cut the fabric and cover the card pieces as for the rectangular tray, adjusting the fabric before stitching the ends to allow for the introduction of the base card (*see* Figs 7.4–7.7).

Measuring and covering the base

For the base, draw a circle on thick card. The radius of this circle must be the radius of the base card used for the box, less one thickness of card. Construct the hexagonal shape and draw a line across the middle to obtain half the shape, as shown in Fig 7.8. Shave off a sliver of card along the diameter equal to the thickness of the card.

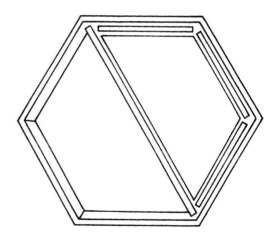

Fig 7.8 **Card arrangement, with base and lining in position, for a hexagonal half tray.**

Check that this base fits inside the tray sides (remember that it will be covered with fabric before being stitched into position) and if necessary adjust accordingly. Draw round this shape onto thin card and cut this card out for the lining. Lace fabric over both pieces of card (*see* Chapter 2, page 12) and stitch them into place on either side of the side seam as for the rectangular tray.

Octagonal Half Tray

The procedure for making a half tray to fit an octagonal box is exactly the same as that for the hexagonal box. (*See* Fig 7.9.)

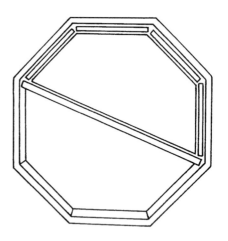

Fig 7.9 **Card arrangement, with base and lining in position, for an octagonal half tray.**

Fig 7.10 **Alternative trays for the octagonal box ready for the covered base to be positioned.**

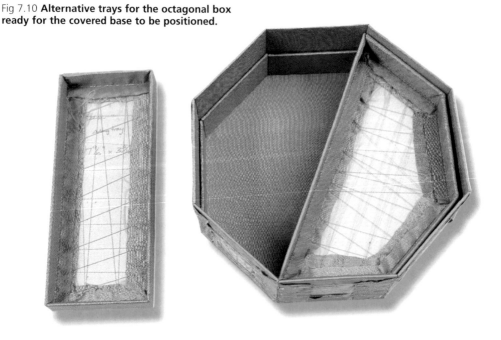

BEFORE
YOU
START

Chapter Eight
Construction methods and planning

Fig 8.1 **The various box components.**

So you have chosen the various elements which dictate the design, size, shape, etc. of the box you intend to make in the planning stage.

There are now a number of choices open to you as regards the method of construction. The choice is entirely personal and will depend on the effect required. Essentially, in this book anyway, there are two distinct alternatives; one will produce a padded effect and the other a tailored style. The quantities of fabric required will differ according to the method chosen.

Planning Check List

**It is a good idea to give consideration to all the
following points before beginning your box.**

1 Is the box to be purely decorative or will it have a function,
such as the storage of sewing items, jewellery, tissues,
handkerchiefs, bits and pieces, etc.?

2 If there is to be embellishment, this should be considered
before starting the box or, at the very least,
the exact dimensions of the decoration should be worked out
so that the box measurements can be calculated accordingly.
Will the decoration be on the lid only or will it also be used
on the sides? (A few suggestions for decorative techniques which
work well on boxes are given in Chapters 22 and 23.)

3 What shape will prove most satisfactory: rectangular,
square, hexagonal, octagonal, round, oval, triangular?

4 What are the ideal overall dimensions for the box?
What type of lid will be employed?
There are various types from which to choose and this will
influence the proportions of the box. (*See* Chapter 3.)

5 Will the lid be hinged and will this need to be held by stays?
(*See* Chapter 4.)

6 Will divisions be helpful?
This will depend on the intended use for the box.
(*See* Chapter 5.)

7 Would a tray (and, consequently, risers to support the tray)
be a useful accessory within the box? (*See* Chapters 6 and 7.)

8 Would a box with drawers serve the intended purpose?
(*See* Chapters 13 and 18.)

The padded box

This is made starting from the inside of the box, i.e., by covering the lining pieces and then padding and covering the carcass. The virtue of this method is that the finished box is lighter, as less card is used in its construction.

The tailored box

The more tailored, double-layer method starts from the outside of the box, constructing the outer layer before adding the linings. This method involves more card cutting and requires great accuracy.

The projects

The following projects illustrate the design and construction of specific boxes using various methods. I hope that you will use your own ideas to vary the size and design of the boxes offered. The use of different fabrics will, of course, alter the whole look of a box and, with the glorious colours and patterns now available, offer an immediate means of making unique boxes.

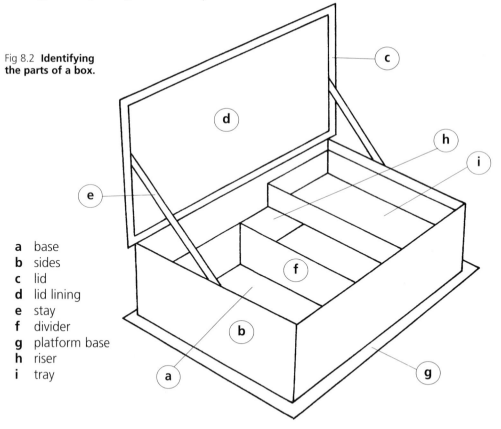

Fig 8.2 **Identifying the parts of a box.**

a   base
b   sides
c   lid
d   lid lining
e   stay
f   divider
g   platform base
h   riser
i   tray

PADDED
BOXES

Chapter Nine
Rectangular boxes

This is a good first box for the beginner to tackle as it employs many basic techniques and will result in a simple, padded rectangular box, 250 x 115 x 65mm (10 x 4½ x 2½in), suitable for the storage of most paper tissues.

Method

Base and sides
Rule out the dimensions of the base and four sides accurately in pencil, on the thick card. Ensure that all the corners are right angles (90°) by using a set square to verify, and check the dimensions carefully before starting to cut the card.

Cut the lining fabric approximately 20mm (¾in) larger all round than each piece of card. Lace each lining piece tightly over the corresponding piece of card, mitring the corners carefully to give a smooth, unwrinkled surface on the covered/unlaced sides of the card. (See Chapter 2, pages 12 and 13.)

Materials

Thick card, for carcass
Thin card, for lining pieces
Lining fabric: approx. ¼m (¼yd)
Felt, thin wadding or similar, for padding
Outer covering fabric: approx.½m (½yd)
Strong thread, for lacing
Thread to match covering fabric or
lining, for sewing

Additional items
Curved needle

Carcass

Place one covered side face to face with the covered base. Line up the corresponding edges, and sew them together through the fabric (*see* Chapter 2, page 14).

Repeat with the remaining sides of the box, attaching each piece to the base before stitching each pair of sides together. This will form the corners to give a firm, neat box base.

Cutting list

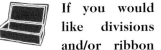

If you would like divisions and/or ribbon stays in the design, they should be considered at this stage. (*See* Chapter 4, for lid stays, and Chapter 5 for dividers.)

Thick card	
Base (cut 1)	250 x 115mm (10 x 4½in)
Long sides (cut 2)	250 x 65mm (10 x 2½in)
Short sides (cut 2)	115 x 65mm (4½ x 2½in)
Hinged lid (cut 1)	265 x 130mm (10½ x 5in)

NB: It is very important that all measurements are precise and that the card is cut accurately.

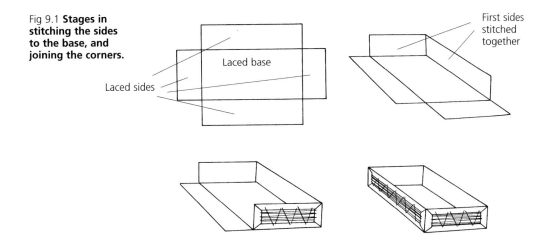

Fig 9.1 **Stages in stitching the sides to the base, and joining the corners.**

Laced base

Laced sides

First sides stitched together

Padding the box carcass

Cut the padding to the exact depth of the box carcass – 65mm (2½in) – and long enough to encircle the base sides with the ends butting together.

Stitch the butted edges of the padding together so that the seam is flat and the padding smooth. You may find it easier to remove the padding from the base for this process: this also helps avoid the possibility of accidentally attaching the padding to the side of the box. (*See* Fig 2.13, page 15.)

If additional padding is required, cut a second piece to fit over the first and stitch in the same way. It is not possible to construct several layers of padding by continuous wrapping around the box as the padding has to be removed at a later stage and it would be difficult to replace this neatly.

Hinge

Using the fabric chosen for the outside covering of the box, cut a strip approximately 75mm (3in) wide and twice the length of the long side which is to be hinged. Fold this in half, right sides together, machine stitch across the end, turn the right sides out and press. This will give a hinge 75mm (3in) wide and just shorter than the inside measurement of the long side of the box to which the hinge will be fixed.

If the available fabric is not the right shape for this, there are alternatives: cut one piece of fabric the same length as the box and 150mm (6in) wide, or two pieces of fabric the same length as the box, each 75mm (3in wide), and stitch accordingly to give a hinge of the required dimensions.

Outer cover

With the padding in place around the carcass, cut a strip of outer covering fabric approximately 50mm (2in) wider than the depth of the box and long enough to wrap around the box with an overlap.

 Bear in mind the pattern of the material, the desirability of centralizing motifs, and the position of the join as it will appear on the outside of the box. (The join in the outer fabric will be least noticeable if it is positioned on a back corner edge.)

With the right side of the fabric against the padding of the box, position the fabric around the carcass and pin the ends closely together over the padding. Ease the material off the box and re-pin 6mm (¼in) *inside* the original position, thus making the cover slightly smaller than before.

Machine or hand stitch firmly along this new line, and press the seam open.

Covering the carcass of the box

Remove the padding from the carcass. Fold the hinge in half lengthways and position it centrally over the back edge of the box, with any pattern upside down (as indicated by the arrows in Fig 9.2). Pin the hinge into position at its edges on the inside and outside of the box, so that the pins are as out of the way as possible.

Take the prepared outer covering, right side out, and stand it the right way up, inside the box, positioning the join at a back corner or as otherwise decided.

Fig 9.2 **Positioning the hinge on the back edge of the box.**

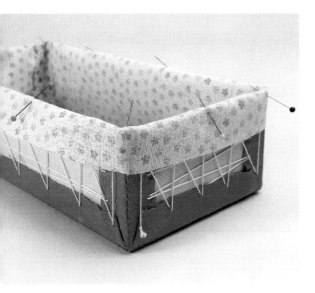

Direction of patterned fabric

Back of box

Pins

With an ordinary sewing thread, sew the outer cover to the base along the top outer edge, using small, even, oversewing stitches. Take care to just catch the lining material underneath, especially when stitching through the hinge fabric as well, where there are four layers of fabric. (Have a look underneath occasionally to check that this is being achieved.)

Fig 9.4 **The required angle of the needle for stitching the cover in place.**

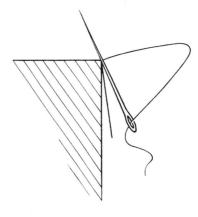

Fig 9.3 **Outer cover positioned inside the box, ready for stitching.**

Fold the cover over the top edge of the box so that approximately 20mm (¾in) extends down the outside of the box, and pin it into place along the top edge. Depending on the type of fabric chosen and the thickness of padding used, it may be necessary to 'ease' the material in order to lose any slight surplus.

Aim to make stitches small and evenly spaced so that they will be almost invisible when the cover is turned out. The gap between these stitches need not be less than 6mm (¼in), but it is important that they are regular to give a neat finish.

Remove all the pins from the base, particularly those holding the hinge, and replace the padding. Turn the cover out and pull it carefully down over the padding, taking care not to move or wrinkle the padding in the process. If it does move or become creased, make sure that any wrinkles are smoothed out. A plastic ruler is useful for smoothing out the padding. Slide the end of the ruler between the padding and the covering fabric and move it about gently, gradually smoothing out any wrinkles.

Pull the material to the underside of the box (checking that it is pulled evenly) and pin it into position.

To lace the covering fabric underneath the box, turn the box upside down. Lace the short sides first, mitring the corners neatly before lacing the long sides, and giving as flat a finish as possible on the undersurface.

By lacing the short sides first, the view of any less-than-perfect mitring is diminished when the finished box is viewed from the front. Keep the lacing stitches as far as possible from the edges of the box to avoid

them showing after the base lining card has been attached.

Finishing the underside

Measure the underside of the box and cut a piece of thin card slightly smaller than this, checking that the angles are 90°. Cut a piece of fabric (either lining material or outer cover as desired) 20mm (¾in) larger all round than this and lace it over the thin card.

 If you are using cereal packaging for this purpose, ensure that the printed side is uppermost when lacing, so that it will not show through the fabric – especially important if a fine fabric is being used.

Fig 9.5 **Outer cover laced under base.**

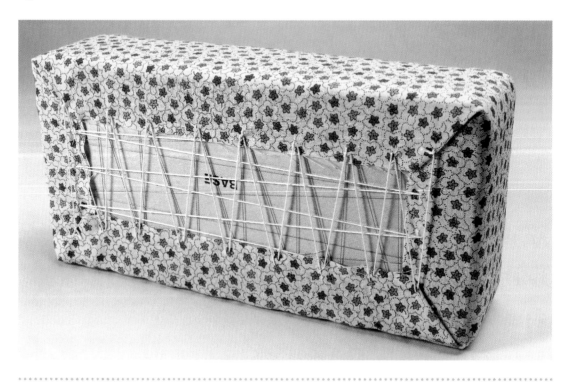

If 'feet' are required, they should be positioned at this stage. Before attaching feet, consider where the box is likely to be placed and if the surface is liable to be scratched by them. Insert split brass paper fasteners through the fabric and card of the base cover, about 20mm (¾in) from the corners. Splay the arms of the fasteners out on the underside.

Fig 9.6 **Positioning the brass feet.**

Pin the covered card into position on the underside of the box, keeping the margins as even as possible all round. Stitch in

place, using ladder stitch and a curved needle. (*See* Chapter 2, pages 13 and 14.)

Lid

For the tissue box shown, the lid dimensions are 265 x 130mm (10½ x 5in). If you are working to your own design, measure the external dimensions of the box top and calculate the dimensions required for the lid, making it approximately 15mm (½in) larger all round. Using these dimensions, mark out the lid accurately onto thick card, check right angles, and cut out.

Cut as many layers of padding as required, exactly the same size as the lid, then cut out the outer fabric, allowing a margin of 40–50mm (1½–2in) all round.

 If you are using a patterned fabric, remember to centralize any motif on the lid. Cut a 'window' in a surplus piece of thin card, and use this to find a good position for the placement of any pattern.

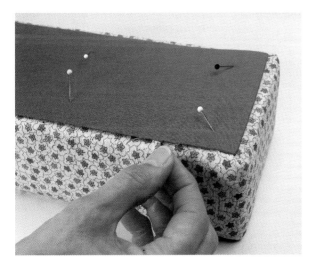

Fig 9.7 **Stitching the base card in place.**

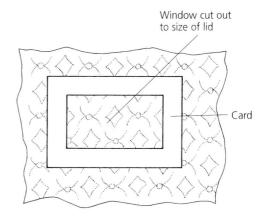

Fig 9.8 **Using a window card to find a suitable pattern area.**

Place the outer fabric on a flat surface, wrong side up, position the padding centrally (checking that any pattern will be correctly positioned), place the lid card on the padding, then pull and pin the outer fabric over the card. Lace the short sides first, making sure that all lacing stitches are well away – at least 20mm (¾in) – from the edges so that they will not show when the lid lining is in position. Mitre carefully (these mitres will show on the corners of the lid), then lace the long sides. The reason for lacing the lid fabric sides in this order is to give a smooth finish along the leading edge of the lid.

For the lid lining, measure the internal dimensions of the box and cut a piece of thin card to these measurements so that it will just fit inside the box after being covered with fabric: this will ensure that it lies inside the top of the box when the lid is closed. Cut a piece of lining fabric 20mm (¾in) larger all round than the card, and lace this over the card, making sure that any printing does not show through the fabric after lacing.

Attaching the lid to the box

Place the box on a firm surface, with the hinge lying inside the box on the far side, and place the lid in position, so that any pattern is the correct way up. Turn the box upside down onto its lid, keeping the hinge on the far side.

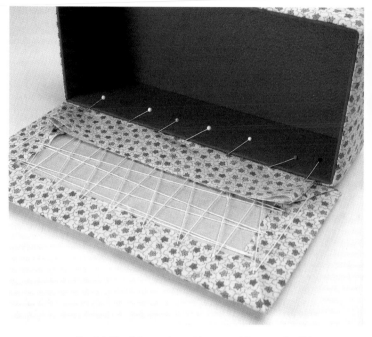

Fig 9.9 **The hinge pinned into position on the lid.**

Looking down from directly above, carefully position the box centrally on its lid. Hold the box firmly with one hand and press down slightly, then gently tilt the box backwards sufficiently to enable the hinge to be seen lying on the underside of the lid.

Slide your other hand in and place it firmly on the hinge. Holding on to the hinge, allow the box to stand vertically, then pin the hinge into position along the back of the lid, as close to the edge of the box as possible.

Position the lining card centrally on the lid, over the hinge, lining it up with the base of the box. Pin it into position, then check, by closing the lid, that it is positioned correctly and that the lining card fits inside the box when the lid is closed.

Fig 9.10 **The lid lining pinned into position.**

When you are satisfied that the lining card is positioned correctly, pin it firmly into position, adding extra pins to ensure that the hinge is securely sandwiched between the lining and the lid. Stitch the lining to the lid, using ladder stitch and a curved needle. Start by stitching along the three unhinged sides. You will then need to use the curved needle in an almost vertical position, making sure that it passes through the hinge and catches the fabric covering the lid as well as the lining, for the fourth side.

If the lid seems to wobble at all, close it, and stitch the underside of its back edge to the hinge to give added strength. Again, use ladder stitch and a curved needle.

Chocolate Box

As a gift for a special occasion (the original model of the box in the photograph was made as a ruby wedding present), this box makes a superb and lasting present since the box of chocolates can be replaced or refilled over and over again.

The base of the box illustrated measures 105 x 210mm (4¼ x 8½in), being approximately 25mm (1in) larger all round than the box of chocolates being housed. The sides are 65mm (2½in) high and the risers 45mm (1¾in) high. The risers were fitted before the sides of the box were stitched together to make the carcass. (For notes on risers *see* Chapter 6.)

Materials

Thick card, for carcass
Thin card, for lining pieces
Lining fabric: approx. ½m (½yd)
Felt, thin wadding or similar, for padding
Outer covering fabric: approx. ½m (½yd)
Strong thread, for lacing
Thread to match covering fabric or
lining, for sewing

Additional items
Curved needle

Method

Follow the instructions given for making a rectangular box (*see* pages 38–45), and choose either a hinged or separate, overlapping lid (*see* Chapter 3). The addition of a platform base might improve the set of this box. (The square boxes shown on page 76 all have platform bases.)

Cut out a piece of thick card to the same dimensions as the base. Position the box of chocolates in the middle of this card and draw round it. (The box shown was made to hold After Eight mints, but boxes can be made to accommodate any chocolates.) Make sure that the corners are right angles before cutting out this portion of card to leave a frame into which the box of chocolates will fit.

To cover the frame with fabric, follow the instructions in Chapter 24, for mounting an embroidery. Place the covered frame in position on the risers and, using ladder stitch with a curved needle, put in just a few stitches in the middle of each side to join the frame to the box; it is unnecessary to stitch all the way round, especially as this would be extremely difficult!

Chapter Ten
Square box

The basic construction of a simple, square box is very similar to the preceding rectangular shape. The resulting box is suitable for the storage of handkerchiefs, small paper napkins or any odds and ends. It measures 135mm (5½in) square and 70mm (2¾in) deep.

Choose the materials for the box carefully, toning or contrasting the outer covering and lining

Cutting list

Thick card

Internal base (cut 1)	135 x 135mm (5½ x 5½in)
Base sides (cut 4)	135 x 70mm (5½ x 2¾in)
Platform base and lid (cut 2)	150 x 150mm (6 x 6in)

Thin card

Lid lining (cut 1)	130 x 130mm (5¼ x 5¼in)

NB: It is very important that all measurements are precise and that the card is cut accurately.

fabrics, and working out any embroidery or other embellishment details (*see* Simple Lid Embellishments, Chapters 22 and 23) before starting to make the box.

Materials

Thick card, for carcass
Thin card, for lining
Lining fabric: approx. ¼m (¼yd)
Felt, thin wadding or similar, for padding
Outer covering fabric: approx. ¼m (¼yd)
Strong thread, for lacing
Thread to match covering fabric or lining, for sewing

Additional items
Curved needle

Method

Rule out the dimensions accurately in pencil on the thick card, ensuring that all the corners are right angles (90°) by using a set square to verify. Check the dimensions carefully before starting to cut the card. As each piece of card is cut, mark the dimensions on it in pencil so that each is clearly identified.

Base and sides
Cut pieces of lining fabric approximately 20mm (¾in) larger all round than each piece of card. Lace each lining piece tightly over the corresponding piece of card, mitring the corners carefully for a smooth, unwrinkled surface on the covered/unlaced side. (*See* Chapter 2, pages 12 and 13.)

Carcass
Place one covered side face to face with one edge of the covered base and sew the edges together through the fabric. (*See* Chapter 2, page 14.) Repeat with the remaining sides of the box, attaching each piece to the base before stitching each pair of sides together to form the corners. This will give a firm, neat box base. (*See* Fig 9.1, page 39.)

Proceed with the construction of this box, following the instructions given for the Rectangular Box (*see* pages 38–42), until the outer cover has been laced underneath the base. If preferred, the lid may be left separate and unhinged, in which case the step to create the hinge should be omitted.

Fig 10.1 **The outer cover positioned in the box prior to folding.**

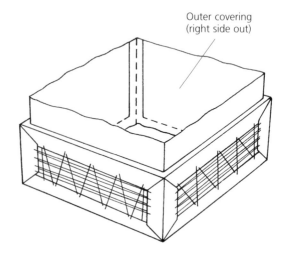

Outer covering
(right side out)

Fig 10.2 **The outer cover ready for stitching.**

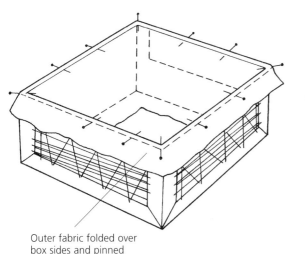

Outer fabric folded over
box sides and pinned

Fig 10.4 **The lid
lining pinned
into position.**

Edges to be stitched

Stitch this edge using the
curved needle vertically –
remove the pins only as
you stitch

Lid

To make the lid, follow the instructions
given for the Rectangular Box (see pages
43–4), using one of the 150mm (6in) square
pieces of thick card. Pad and decorate the
lid as desired. Either leave this as a separate
unit or attach it to the box following the
hinging instructions given for the Rectangular
Box (see pages 40–5).

Base platform

Take the remaining piece of 150mm (6in)
square thick card and cut a piece of outer
covering fabric, 20mm (¾in) larger all round.

Lace the card with fabric and place laced
side up on a firm surface. Position the box
centrally on this card, pin it firmly in place,
and stitch the edge of the box to the fabric
covering the base platform using ladder
stitch with a curved needle.

Fig 10.3 **The hinge
pinned into position
on the lid.**

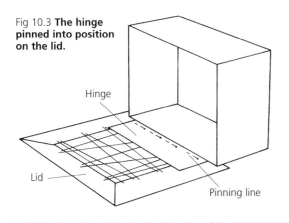

Hinge

Lid

Pinning line

Chapter Eleven
Hexagonal and octagonal boxes

H exagonal and octagonal boxes offer neat and interesting alternatives to boxes with right-angled corners and make attractive sewing or jewellery boxes as they can be compartmentalized by putting in divisions or adding risers and trays.

Hexagonal Box

Method

Base

Decide on the maximum width (corner to corner) for the base of the box. This will be the diameter of the circle which needs to be drawn in order to mark out the hexagonal shape.

Using a pair of compasses set at half the desired width dimension for the box base, draw a circle on a piece of thick card. Keeping the same radius, place the point of your compass on the circumference of the circle and mark the points at which the pencil cuts the circle on either side (see Fig 11.1).

Fig 11.1 **The first arcs on the circumference, using the compasses.**

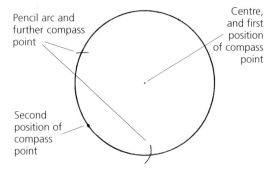

Pencil arc and further compass point

Centre, and first position of compass point

Second position of compass point

Materials

Thick card, for carcass
Thin card, for lining pieces
Lining fabric
Felt, thin wadding or similar, for padding
Outer covering fabric
Strong thread, for lacing
Thread to match covering fabric or
lining, for sewing

Additional items
Curved needle
Protractor
Pair of compasses

Move the point of your compasses to one of the pencil marks and repeat the procedure. Doing this all round the circumference will give you six evenly spaced marks. Draw lines joining these points and cut out the resulting hexagon.

Fig 11.2 **The six arcs.**

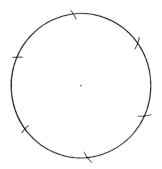

Alternatively, place a protractor in the centre of the circle, at the mark made by the point of the compasses and, with a pencil, mark off 60° angles, then rule lines

from the centre to the circumference at these angles. This will divide the circle into six segments. Join the six points where the lines cut the circumference to form the hexagon and cut out the resulting shape.

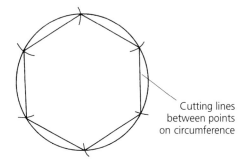

Cutting lines
between points
on circumference

Fig 11.3 **The hexagon formed by joining the six marks.**

Sides

Six side panels are required to make the box. The length of each matches the radius of the initial circle, and the height should equal the depth required for the box. Mark out these six panels accurately on the thick card, in pencil, check that the angles are 90°, and cut out.

Lid

Using the same method as for the base, draw and cut out a flat lid, making the radius of the initial circle slightly larger than that used for the base. This gives an overlap, making it easy to open the box.

Proceed with the construction of the box as for the Rectangular Box in Chapter 9, lacing the lining fabric over the base and the side pieces and stitching them together. (*See* pages 38–45.)

The lid can be hinged in the same way as

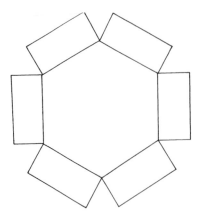

Fig 11.4 **The base with the side panels attached.**

Fig 11.5 **The base, ready to be padded and covered.**

for a rectangular box, but stays will certainly be required to hold the lid in a stable open position, since any hinge will be small in proportion to the size of the box. (*See* Chapter 3 for alternative lid designs and Chapter 4 for lid stays.)

Octagonal Box Method

Base

As for a hexagonal box, you must first decide on the maximum width (corner to corner) for your box in order to set the diameter of the circle required to mark out the octagonal shape. Using compasses set at half the desired width dimension, draw a circle on a thick piece of card. Draw a line across the centre of this circle and then, using a protractor or a set square, draw a second line at right angles to the first. Divide each of the resulting quarters in half by drawing two more lines across the centre of the circle, thus dividing the circle into eight equal segments.

Draw lines joining these points and cut out the resulting octagonal shape to make the base of the box.

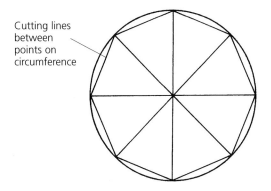

Cutting lines between points on circumference

Fig 11.6 **The octagon formed by joining the eight marks.**

Sides

Measure the sides of the octagonal base (they should all be the same) and, using this measurement for the length and the desired height of the box for the width, mark out the eight side pieces on thick card, in pencil. Check that the angles are 90°, and cut out.

Proceed with the construction of the carcass as for the Hexagonal Box (*see* pages 50–2).

Lid

Using the same method as for the base, draw and cut out a flat lid, making the radius for the initial circle slightly larger than that used in the construction of the base. Hinging the lid is optional, but as the hinge will be relatively narrow, it may prove preferable to add a lid which is not hinged. Where a hinge is too narrow in proportion to the size and weight of the lid, it will be lacking in strength and the lid will wobble about too much. Alternative lid designs are given in Chapter 3.

Chapter Twelve
Round and oval boxes

Whilst slightly more demanding in their early stages of construction, round and oval boxes are most satisfactory to make and create attractive finished products. The first step is to decide on the shape and size of the proposed box (round, oval, curve-ended), and the type of lid to be used. (*See* Chapter 3 for alternative lid styles and read these instructions before proceeding any further.)

Divisions and trays can also be designed for rounded boxes: in this case, the risers and the inner lining sides and base should be joined together and the divisions put in place before the linings are attached to the inside of the box.

Materials

Thick card, for carcass
Thin card, for lining
Lining fabric
Felt, thin wadding or similar, for padding
Outer covering fabric
Strong thread, for lacing
Thread to match covering fabric or
lining, for sewing

Additional items
Curved needle
Pair of compasses
Masking tape

Method

Marking out the base

You will probably be able to find a plate or dish to draw around; if not, you will need to construct the required shape using a pair of compasses. (Round and oval boxes, and even other curved shapes, may be made using thin, ready-cut cake boards for the base and lid. These are readily available and make life very much easier!)

For marking out round and oval boxes, refer to Fig 12.1.

For curve-ended boxes, draw the dimensions of the rectangle which will form the basis of the curve-ended shape on to a piece of thick card. Measure and mark the halfway point between the long sides. This measurement (to the halfway point) is equal to the radius required for the semi-circles giving the curved ends. Using the mark as the centre of the circle, draw the semicircles to make the ends of the box.

 For more complicated designs the base can be marked and cut out and the sides moulded in the same way as that described on page 56. The lids for such designs should be carefully considered: a drop-in lid would allow the shape to be cut out at the same time as the base (*see* Alternative lid designs, page 60).

Cutting out the base

Having drawn the required shape on thick card, cut it out. A 'compass cutter' eases the problem of cutting circles, incorporating as it does a blade instead of a pencil to cut a circle in card.

Alternatively, use a Stanley knife or similar craft knife with a sharp blade. Press very carefully and lightly for the first

Fig 12.1 **Constructing different rounded shapes.**

Centre points of circles for
constructing curved ends

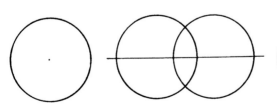
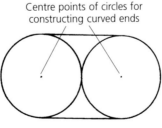
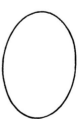

circuit, allowing the blade to follow the groove already made by the pencil, then gradually increase the pressure until the shape is cleanly cut, following the deepening groove. When cutting, always keep the knife blade upright.

 If a drop-in lid (*see* Fig 3.6) or a lid with a framing lip over a rising lining (*see* Fig 3.11) is planned, cut a second piece of card, the same as the base, at this stage.

Covering the base

If padding is required on the bottom of the box, cut a piece of felt or similar, using the card as a template.

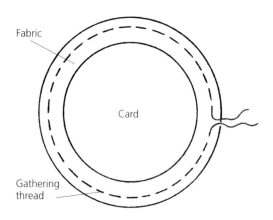

Fig 12.2 **The gathering thread positioned round the outer edge of the fabric to cover the base.**

For the covering, cut a piece of fabric, allowing 25mm (1in) turnings all round, and put in a gathering thread 15mm (½in) from the outer edge. Place the base card (padded side down if applicable) on the wrong side of the fabric as shown in Fig 12.2. Pull up the

gathering thread, tightening the fabric over the card at the same time, then pin into position, easing the fullness evenly, and lace. (*See* Fig 12.3.)

Fig 12.3 **Pinning and lacing the gathered fabric over the base.**

Cutting and moulding the box side

In order to achieve the curve required for the sides of round and oval boxes, the card must be dampened and moulded. As you will find, a sheet of card will bend more easily in one direction than another, so cut lengthwise accordingly.

Cut a strip of card of a width to match the required height and slightly longer than the circumference of the base. Place the covered base in a polythene bag and seal, excluding the air.

Dampen the strip of card on both sides with a wet sponge to make it pliable and bend it carefully around the base. Using string, elastic bands or tape, fix the card into position and leave to dry – allow 24 hours.

When the card is completely dry, remove

Fig 12.4 **The box side tied to hold it in shape.**

the ties. Trim the strip of card to the exact size, butting the edges and using masking tape or similar to fasten the join (*see* Fig 12.5).

 If the box is to have a lid with an under lip placed over a rising lining (*see* Fig 3.10), both the lid and the lip can be made now. Cut a second circle of card for the top, the same size as the base, and a long strip of card for the sides. This strip should have a width equal to the depth of lip required and be slightly longer than the circumference of the lid. Mould this around the covered lid in the same way.

Padding the box side

Cut a strip of padding (felt, wadding or similar) to the same width as the side and long enough to fit around the outside of the box. Position and smooth the padding, butting and stitching the edges together. (*See* Chapter 2, page 14, and Fig 12.5.)

Covering the box side

Cut a strip of fabric 50mm (2in) wider than the height of the box and, with the right side of the fabric facing the box side, wrap the fabric tightly around the box, pinning the fabric together where the two 'ends' meet. Ease the fabric off the padded side, and stitch the sides together just inside the pinned seam. Turn and press the seam.

Fig 12.5 **The shaped, taped and padded card for the side, awaiting covering.**

With the padding in position, and with the right side of the covering fabric now facing out, reposition the covering fabric on the box side. Making sure that the padding remains in position, pull the fabric evenly over the top and bottom edges to the inside of the box. Pin and lace the fabric firmly on the inside of the box. (*See* Fig 12.6.)

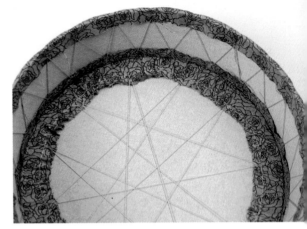

Fig 12.7 **The base and sides joined together.**

Fig 12.6 **Fabric laced inside the box side.**

Attaching the sides to the base
Place the covered side over the base (laced surface uppermost inside the box) and ladder stitch together on the underside, using a curved needle and matching thread.

Cutting and covering the base lining
Cut a circle of thin card (the same radius as the original base card) to fit inside the box. Cut a circle of fabric 25mm (1in) larger all round than the card. If any padding, quilting, embroidery or other decoration is desired, it should be worked at this stage, before lacing the fabric over the card as for the base. (*See* Fig 12.3.) Drop the covered base lining into position in the box, lace

side down. While I don't recommend using glue on fabric, I do use a glue stick to stick the two card surfaces together. Use only a very small amount of glue and leave it to dry thoroughly under pressure.

Lining the box
The height of the lining will depend on the design of the chosen lid. For a lid with a lip, a rising lining is required. This lining should rise above the side of the box by 10–25mm (½–1in), depending, of course, on the proportions of the box. For a drop-in or overlapping lid, the lining should stop approximately 6mm (¼in) below the height of the box. (*See* Figs 12.8 and 12.9.)

According to the box design, cut a strip of thin card to the required height and long enough to fit around the inside of the box. Place this strip inside the box and cut to fit, overlapping the card slightly. Join the ends using masking tape. The card will be covered with lining fabric so allow for this by not making the lining fit too tightly.

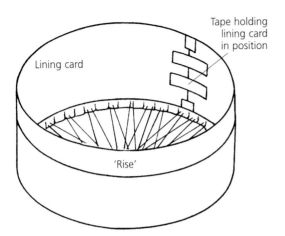

Fig 12.8 **Rising lining.**

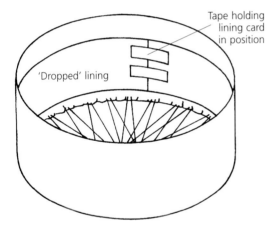

Fig 12.9 **Lining below the lip of the box.**

Cut a strip of lining fabric, the width of which should be 25mm (1in) less than twice the height of the lining card and the length enough to wrap around it with an overlap of about 25mm (1in). Turn in one end of the strip and pin it onto the card then pin the strip into position inside the lining card; if the lining is to rise above the box side, allow more of the fabric to overlap at the top edge of the card than the lower edge. (*See* Fig 12.10.)

Fig 12.10 **Lining fabric pinned into position.**

Turn the fabric out over the upper and lower edges of the card and lace it into position on the outside, easing and smoothing the fabric inside the card in the process. When the lacing is complete, turn the other end of the fabric in to butt tightly against the first, and ladder stitch the two edges together, using a curved needle.

Fig 12.11 **Attaching the rising lining to the box.**

Fig 12.12 **Attaching the below-lip lining to the box.**

Position the covered lining inside the box on top of the base lining, which it will hold in place, and ladder stitch to the outer cover along the top edge, using a curved needle. (*See* Figs 12.11 and 12.12.)

Alternative Lid Designs

Lid with framing lip

This design is suitable for a box that has been made with a rising lining. (*See* Lids with lips, Chapter 3, page 18.)

Cut out the required shape for the lid in thick card, using the same radius as for the original box base. Cut the fabric for the lid, then gather and lace as for the base of the box. (*See* Covering the base and Fig 12.3, page 56.)

 Any decoration – embroidery, patchwork and quilting – should be carried out before the lid fabric is laced over the card.

Cut a card strip to the required lip depth and long enough to go around the covered lid. Place the covered lid inside a polythene bag, excluding any air, then dampen and mould the strip of card around it as for the box side. (*See* Cutting and moulding the box side and Fig 12.4, pages 56 and 57.) Fix the side into position and leave to dry for 24 hours. When dry, trim the strip of card to size, butt the edges and join using masking tape.

If the sides of the box have been padded, pad the lip to the same thickness.

Cut a piece of outer fabric twice the depth of the card plus 40mm (1½in). (If the fabric covering the base has been cut on the cross, then the fabric covering the lip must also be cut this way.) With the right side out, turn in one end of the fabric strip and pin in position on the lip so that the fabric can be folded under and up to cover both sides of the card. Position the strip of fabric all round the lip, turning in the second edge at the join. Either by hand or machine (using a zip foot), stitch all round the fabric, close to the card (see Fig 12.13). Ladder stitch the fabric seam.

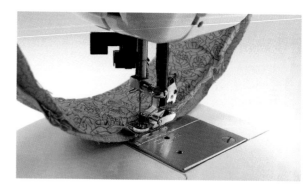

Fig 12.13 **Stitching the fabric over the card for the framing lip.**

To allow the covered lid to sit inside the lip, the seam must be pulled down sufficiently inside the lip. Once you have eased the seam down and positioned the lid, ladder stitch the lid inside the lip, using a curved needle. (*See* Fig 12.14.)

Fig 12.14 **Stitching the lid inside the framing lip using a curved needle.**

To line the lid, cut the required shape in thin card using the same radius as the lid. Cut the same shape in fabric, 40mm (1½in) larger than the card all round. Work any quilting, embroidery or other decoration, if desired, at this stage. Pad the card if required, then gather and lace lining fabric over the card as for base. (*See* Covering the base and Fig 12.3, page 56.)

Using a small amount of glue between the card surfaces, position the lid lining, and allow to dry under pressure.

Lid with under lip

For this lid arrangement, the first procedure is to cut and mould the lip in the same way as for the box sides (*see* page 56). The dimensions for the top are then obtained from this lip.

Cover the lip as described for a lid with a framing lip (*see* Fig 12.13), but this time the seam should be pulled at right angles to the card to allow the lid to sit on top (*see* Fig 12.14).

To find the radius for the lid top, measure across the lip. To accommodate any slight loss of shape measure twice, taking the second measurement at right angles to the first. Find the mean of these two measurements, and divide this by two to obtain the radius: cut out the appropriate card circle.

 If any decoration, such as embroidery, patchwork or quilting is desired, it should be worked before the lid is covered.

Pad, cover and lace the fabric over this card as previously described (*see* Covering the base and Fig 12.3). Position the covered card on top of the lip and stitch the lip to the underside, using ladder stitch and a curved needle. (*See* Fig 12.15.)

For the lining, cut a circle of thin card to fit inside the lip of the lid – the radius for this should be the same as that for the original box base. Pad and cover this thin card, quilting or decorating as required.

Using a small amount of glue between the card surfaces, position the lid lining inside the lid and allow to dry under pressure.

Fig 12.15 **Stitching the lid to the under lip.**

Drop-in lid

To accommodate this type of lid, the lining for the box is constructed to stop 6mm (¼in) below the top edge of the box. (*See* Chapter 3, page 18.) The radius of the card circle required for the lid is the same as the radius of the base card.

 The fabric for the lid should be padded, embroidered, quilted, or otherwise decorated, if any decoration is desired, before being positioned and laced over the card in the same way as for the base. (*See* **Covering the base and Fig 12.3, page 56.**)

Fit some form of handle, covered button or tassel to the centre of the lid, fastening it through the card and finishing off underneath, where it will be covered by the lining.

The thin lining card for this type of lid should be cut so that, when the lid rests on the box lining, the lid lining fits closely inside the box lining. Measure the internal dimension of the box and cut the lid lining card accordingly, allowing for the fabric covering. Pad if required and cover in the usual way, then ladder stitch into position underneath the lid, around the edge of the lining, using a curved needle.

Pop-on flat lid

As with a drop-in lid, to accommodate this type of lid, the lining for the box is constructed to stop 6mm (¼in) below its top edge. (*See* Chapter 3, page 17.) A pop-on lid can be made to finish flush with the sides of the box or allowed to overlap, extending beyond them: having made this decision, calculate the radius required.

Draw, cut and cover the card as previously described for the base card. (*See* Covering the base and Fig 12.3, page 56.)

Cut the thin card for the lid lining, using the same radius as that for the base card of the box. Cover with fabric, as described for the lid designs above, and ladder stitch into position around the edge of the lining card, using a curved needle.

Fig 12.16 **Round, oval and curve-ended boxes with different types of lid.**

Fig 12.17 **One box style with three different lids.**

Chapter Thirteen
Chest of drawers

This is a most versatile box which can be built up in various combinations of short and long drawers, making it a useful addition to any room, for a myriad of storage purposes, including jewellery, stationery, handkerchiefs, and writing materials.

Using a contrasting plain fabric for the casings of the drawers gives a very pleasing effect to the finished product.

Materials

Thick card, for carcass
Thin card, for lining
Lining fabric
Felt, thin wadding or similar, for padding
Outer covering fabric
Strong thread, for lacing
Thread to match covering fabric or
lining, for sewing
Drawer pulls or tabs, as required
(buttons, ribbons, etc.)

Additional items
Curved needle

Method

Calculating dimensions

Boxes with drawers are usually built up starting with the construction of the drawers, then the drawer casings, and finally the outer casing forming the actual box. Where this is the case, it is important to decide on the overall maximum dimensions of the box in the design stage, and then to work backwards with the approximate calculations so as to establish the size of the drawers.

 In taking measurements and cutting card, always make allowances for the thickness of the fabric, turnings and lacings.

Decide on the design of the overall box and any decoration for the outer casing (top or sides) or the drawer fronts, on the number of drawers to be included and on the method to be used for opening them.

The simplest design to make is one that has all the drawers the same size: in this case, the card pieces for the basic drawers can and should all be cut at the same time. For a box which involves drawers of more than one size, start with the construction of the short drawers, which will ultimately dictate the dimensions of the longer drawers.

Establish the overall size of the 'chest of drawers' and make an approximate calculation for the shorter drawers.

Fig 13.1 **Alternative simple drawer combinations.**

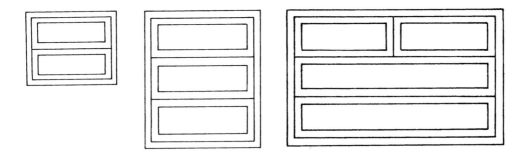

Short Drawers

Sides

Cut the sides of the drawer in thick card, so that the front and back pieces lie across the shorter sides and provide a smooth, unbroken front to the drawer.

Number the side pieces, starting with the back and working in either direction. Cut a piece of covering fabric twice the depth of the card pieces, plus a little extra for seam allowance. Lay the pieces in a line on the fabric, in numerical order, as shown in Fig 13.3.

Fold the edges in and pin the fabric tightly against the card. Stitch the seam close to the card either by hand, using a back stitch, or using the zip foot of a machine (*see* Chapter 2, page 15; *see also* Figs 7.5 and 7.6).

After stitching, pull the fabric round the card until the seam is far enough round to allow for a covered base card to be inserted

underneath and lie flush with the lower edges of the sides of the drawer. (*See* Fig 7.7.)

Ladder stitch across the fabric close to each end of the card pieces so that they are all safely contained. Fold the fabric into a drawer shape, then ladder stitch the two ends together, making sure that the pieces of card are lying correctly beside one another (*see* Fig 13.2).

Fig 13.3 **Card pieces positioned on the fabric for the drawer sides.**

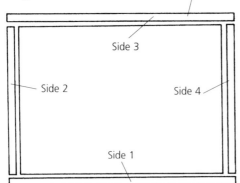

Fig 13.2 **Plan view of the card arrangement for a drawer.**

Base

Measure across the drawer sides to establish the dimensions of the base required. Mark and cut out the base in thick card: the short edge will be the same as the short side of the drawer and the long side will be the length of the drawer's long side minus two thicknesses of card. Check that the right angles are accurate and that the base will fit neatly, allowing for its fabric covering.

 If a tab method of opening the drawer is to be employed, stitch the chosen ribbon into position at the front, inside the drawer, before introducing the base.

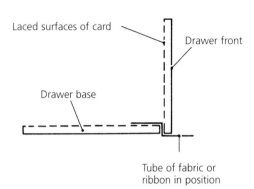

Fig 13.4 **Positioning the fabric pull tab.**

Cut out the outer covering fabric and lace it over the base card in the usual way. Introduce it from below, laced face upwards, to complete the outside of the drawer and ladder stitch into place from below, using a curved needle. The drawer will now be stable.

Cut a piece of thin card to the same dimensions as the drawer base. Cover this by lacing with the lining fabric (which may first be padded, quilted, embroidered, etc.). Lightly glue the laced surface of this card and position it in the drawer: it should fit snugly and hide the seam allowance in the drawer, which should be made as flat as possible. Leave to dry under pressure.

Drawer casings

A casing must be made for each drawer and these casings then ladder stitched together, using a curved needle. To do this, measure the outer dimensions of the drawer and cut thick card for the casing accordingly. When calculating the length of the sides of the casing, add one thickness of card to the length of the drawer to allow for a piece of covered card to be inserted at the back of the casing. Card for the casings of other drawers of the same dimensions should be cut simultaneously.

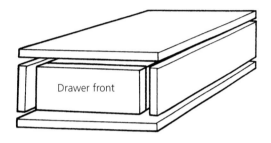

Fig 13.5 **Assembly of card for outer casing.**

Lace fabric over each of the card pieces, then ladder stitch them together, with laced surfaces on the outside, ensuring that the correct alignment is maintained.

Fig 13.6 **Inserting the back panel into the casing.**

With the drawer in position to stabilize the casing, measure for the back panel insert, allowing for it to be covered with fabric. Cut the card, lace with fabric and place in position inside the casing with the laced surface outside. Ladder stitch into place, using a curved needle.

Drawer handle

A handle for opening the drawer should be attached through the front of the drawer once the base has been stitched in place. Stitch a patch of matching fabric over the fixing on the inside if necessary.

Fig 13.7 **Attaching a drawer facing.**

Alternative drawer facing and handle

To avoid the handle fixing showing on the inside of the drawer, a drawer-front facing may be made separately. The dimensions for this facing can only be established once the drawer casing has been constructed, since this facing must cover the casing exactly.

Once you have determined the dimensions of the facing, cut and lace fabric over the card in the usual way. Fix the handle through the facing before attaching it to the front of the drawer, by ladder stitching with a curved needle. (*See* page 85 for a method of attaching a button with a shank as a drawer pull.)

Long Drawers

In this design, the dimensions for the casings of the long drawers are determined by the casings of the shorter drawers. Ladder stitch these together side by side and measure carefully to find the dimensions for the long drawers.

Fig 13.8 **Finding the dimensions of the long drawer casing.**

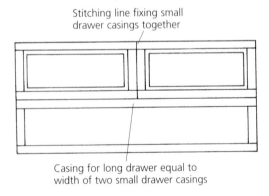

Stitching line fixing small drawer casings together

Casing for long drawer equal to width of two small drawer casings

 Where the order of construction allows, it is easier to have the drawers in position when stitching the casings together, as this gives greater stability.

In this case, it is necessary to construct the casings for the long drawers first and then make the drawers themselves to fit inside, calculating the dimensions from the casing. Remember at all times to allow for the thickness of the fabric.

Outer casing

Once all the drawers and their casings have been assembled, ladder stitch all the casings securely together. An outer casing can then be constructed.

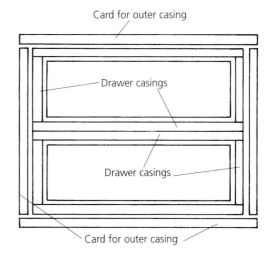

Card for outer casing

Drawer casings

Drawer casings

Card for outer casing

Fig 13.10 **The card arrangement for the outer casing, viewed from the front.**

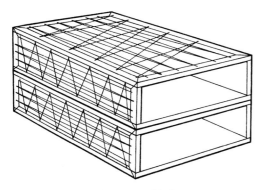

Fig 13.9 **Drawer casings assembled, ready for stitching together.**

Take the measurements for the outer casing in exactly the same way as for the single drawer casing but, when you ladder stitch them together, have the laced surfaces facing the inside. Remember to allow for the introduction of a panel at the back of the outer casing.

If preferred, the card for the top of the box can be cut to overlap and the base card can be cut larger to act as a platform. To attach an overlapping top or base, use ladder stitch and a curved needle.

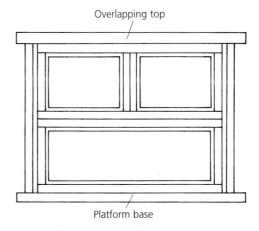

Overlapping top

Platform base

Fig 13.11 **Alternative finish for the outer casing.**

DOUBLE-LAYER BOXES

Chapter Fourteen
Pen holder

This is the simplest double-layer box and a neat answer to the permanent question 'Where are the pens?' It can be made up in fabrics to co-ordinate with the Letter Rack on page 73 to make a stylish display on a desk or table, perhaps near the telephone.

Method

Cutting and covering the sides

If you are inserting decorated panels, work these first and mount them, then construct the pen holder according to the dimensions of the finished mount. (*See* Chapter 24, page 111, for advice on mounting the work.) Otherwise, when making a simple, fabric-covered pen holder, start by cutting four identical pieces of card to the required dimensions of the pen holder sides. The sides of the box shown measure 160 x 80mm (6 x 3in). Pad and lace the card with outer fabric.

Materials

Thick card, for carcass
Thin card, for lining
Fabric, the same for both outer
covering and lining

Additional items
Curved needle
Iron-on interfacing and double-sided
tape, if mounting any decoration

Assembling and lining the sides

Following the arrangement of the pieces of covered card as indicated in Fig 14.1, ladder stitch the outer sides together, using a curved needle. Measure the internal dimensions (allowing for fabric covering), cut four thin card pieces to fit and lace with fabric.

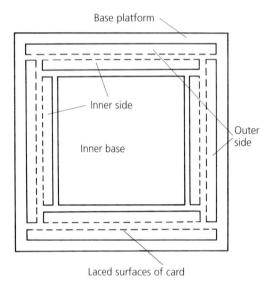

Fig 14.1 **Plan view of card arrangement for pen holder.**

Insert and stitch the lining cards into position, one by one, starting with the larger pieces on opposite sides. To assemble, ladder stitch each piece to the appropriate outer side along the top edge, using a curved needle.

Fitting the platform and inner base

Cut a piece of card 6mm (¼in) larger all round than the outer base of the pen holder and lace with fabric: this forms the platform base. Ensure that there is a good margin of fabric outside the lacing stitches. Position the pen holder on the laced surface of the base, and stitch into position all round, using ladder stitch and a curved needle.

Finally, cut a piece of thin card to the dimensions of the inner base of the pen holder and lace with fabric. With the laced surface down, push the card to the base of the holder: it will not require stitching.

Chapter Fifteen
Letter rack

Method

If you wish to incorporate a decorated panel, follow the suggestions for mounting given in Chapter 24 (*see* page 111). Otherwise, for a simple, fabric-covered box, cut card in accordance with personal choice. The overall dimensions of the letter rack shown are 215mm (8½in) high, 265mm (10½in) wide, and 130mm (5in) deep.

A perfect partner for the Pen Holder, this useful rack can be used for stationery, such as notepaper and envelopes, or to hold letters and stamps. Choose a fabric to co-ordinate with room furnishings or to pick up a particular colour and decide what size rack is required. The measurements given in the instructions are for the letter rack illustrated.

Materials

Thick card, for carcass
Thin card, for lining
Fabric, the same for both outer covering and lining
Iron-on interfacing
Padding, if required

Additional items
Curved needle

Side panels

Cut two pieces of L-shaped card in accordance with Fig 15.1. Next, cut two pieces of fabric and two pieces of firm, iron-on interfacing 20mm (¾in) larger all round. Iron the interfacing onto the wrong side of the fabric and lace the fabric pieces over the card, cutting carefully into the corners for neatness.

Following the arrangement of the pieces of covered card as indicated in Figs 15.2 and 15.3, join the four completed outer sides together, using ladder stitch and a curved needle. Note that the front lining is stitched with its laced surface facing outwards.

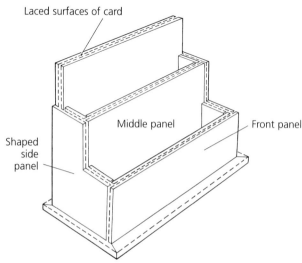

Fig 15.2 **Assembling the letter rack.**

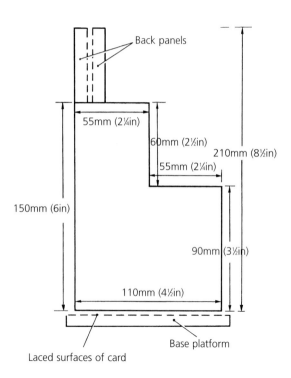

Fig 15.1 **Side view of letter rack.**

Front and back panels

Cut pieces of card to the desired size for the two back panels and front inner panels. Lace fabric over each of the three pieces. Ladder stitch the two back pieces together, laced sides facing.

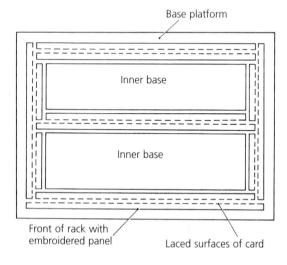

Fig 15.3 **Plan view of letter rack.**

Cut a piece of thick card for the front of the rack, pad if required, lace with fabric and stitch into place using ladder stitch and a curved needle.

Inner panels

Cut a card panel to fit the middle of the rack and lace with fabric. Ladder stitch the upper part of this card at either end to the top sections of the L-shaped side panels, using a curved needle.

Measure the internal dimensions of the rack then cut thin card for the four inner sides and lace with fabric. You can now find the dimensions for the 'inner' middle panel: cut and cover thin card for this panel and stitch in place as before.

Inner and outer base

Cut a piece of thick card 10mm (½in) larger all round than the outer base of the letter rack. Lace this card with fabric to use as a platform base.

Position the letter rack on the laced surface of the platform and stitch all round, using ladder stitch and a curved needle.

To finish the rack, cut pieces of thin card to the dimensions of the two inner bases and lace them with fabric. With the laced surfaces underneath, push each piece down inside the appropriate section: stitching is not required.

Chapter Sixteen
Square box

Method

Rule out the dimensions carefully in pencil on the thick card, ensuring that all the corners are right angles by using a set square to verify. Check the dimensions carefully before starting to cut the card. As each piece of card is cut, mark the dimensions on it in pencil to avoid any pieces becoming confused.

T his small, square box is suitable for the storage of handkerchiefs, tissues or any collected odds and ends. The external dimensions are approximately 140mm (5½in) square and the top and base 155mm (6in) square.

Choose the materials for your box carefully, toning or contrasting the fabrics for the outer covering and lining and working out any embroidery or other embellishment details before starting to make the box. The instructions which follow, and the dimensions given, are based on the illustrated boxes.

Materials

Thick card, for carcass
Thin card, for lining
Lining fabric: approx. ¼m (¼yd)
Thin wadding: 155mm (6in) square
Outer covering fabric: approx. ¼m (¼yd)
Strong thread, for lacing
Thread to match covering fabric or lining, for sewing

Additional items
Curved needle

Cutting list

Thick card

Internal base (cut 1)	130 x 130mm (5 x 5in)
Internal sides (cut 2)	130 x 70mm (5 x 2¾in)
Internal sides (cut 2)	135 x 70mm (5¼ x 2¾in)
External sides (cut 2)	135 x 70mm (5¼ x 2¾in)
External sides (cut 2)	140 x 70mm (5½ x 2¾in)
Platform base and lid (cut 2)	155 x 155mm (6 x 6in)

Thin card

Lid lining	130 x 130mm (5 x 5in)

NB: It is very important that all measurements are precise and that the card is cut accurately.

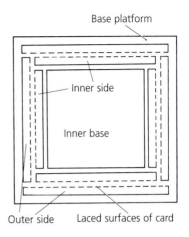

Fig 16.1 **Plan view of card arrangement for square box.**

Inner sides and base

Cut the pieces of lining fabric approximately 20mm (¾in) larger all round than the corresponding pieces of card, and lace each piece tightly over the card, mitring the corners carefully for a smooth, unwrinkled surface on the covered/unlaced side. (*See* Chapter 2, pages 12 and 13.)

Position the sides carefully, as shown in Fig 16.1 and, using a curved needle, ladder stitch them together, laced surfaces out. Introduce the inner base, laced face down, and stitch this into place from below.

Outer sides

Cut pieces of outer covering fabric, again approximately 20mm (¾in) larger all round than the corresponding pieces of card, and lace the fabric over the outer side card pieces. Stitch these to the inner sides of the box, in the correct positions and with the laced surfaces facing, along the top edges and down the sides.

Lid

If you have worked a piece of embroidery, patchwork or some similar decoration which requires 'mounting', a method of framing and mounting is recommended in Chapter 24, page 111.

If no decoration is involved, use a piece of card 155mm (6in) square and pad with a piece of thick wadding cut to the same dimensions. It may be necessary to cut several layers of padding to achieve the effect you want. Cut a piece of outer covering fabric 200mm (8in) square, place this wrong side up, on a flat surface, then position the felt and the card on top.

 If you are using a patterned fabric, remember to centre any motif. Cut a 'window', 155mm (6in square), in a piece of surplus thin card and use this to find a good position for any pattern on the lid.

Lace the outer fabric firmly over the card, making sure that all lacing stitches are well away – at least 15mm (⅝in) – from the edges, so that these stitches will not show after the lid lining is in position. Mitre the corners carefully – these mitres will show.

Next, take the thin piece of card, 130mm (5in) square, and lace a piece of lining fabric, 155mm (6in) square, over it. Make sure any printing on this card does not show through the fabric.

Position the lining card on the laced surface of the lid and pin into position. Check, by placing the lid on the box, that the lining card will fit inside the box when the lid is closed. Once this is done, pin the lining card firmly into position, then stitch the lining to the lid, using ladder stitch and a curved needle.

Base platform

Take the remaining piece of thick card, 155mm (6in) square, and cut a piece of outer covering fabric, 200mm (8in) square. Lace the card with fabric as before, making sure that the lacing is kept well in from the edges of the card so that no stitches will show when the box is in position. Place this card, laced side up, on a firm surface. Position the box centrally on this card, pinning it firmly in place, and stitch the edge of the box to the fabric covering the base platform, using ladder stitch and a curved needle.

Chapter Seventeen
Triangular box

The idea for this box came from my need for a container on my dressing table into which I could put lots of odds and ends but which, at the same time, would remain relatively organized *and* be decorative. This triangular box, with its four compartments, serves the purpose admirably: the box also fits neatly into an awkward space.

You can choose to leave the box uncovered, to have separate lids for each triangular compartment, or to make one large lid to cover the whole box. The dimensions given in the instructions refer to a box with outer side pieces of 255mm (10in).

Materials

Thick card, for carcass
Thin card, for lining
Set square with 60°/30° angles
Lining fabric
Outer covering fabric
Strong thread, for lacing
Thread to match covering fabric or lining, for sewing
Buttons, beads or similar, for lid knobs

Additional items
Curved needle

Method

Small Triangles

Begin by constructing the four small triangular boxes. The three outer triangles use the main fabric for the sides and contrast fabric for the linings, whilst the central triangle reverses this.

It is important to rule out and mark accurately in pencil, the dimensions of the box you are going to make. Ensure that, where called for, all the card corners are right angles, using the right angle of the set square to check each one. In this case, it is also important that the angles of the triangles, when made up, are all 60°. Always double-check the dimensions carefully before starting to cut the card.

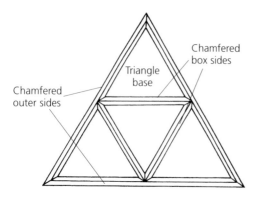

Fig 17.1 **Plan view of card arrangement for triangular box with four small triangular inserts.**

Sides

For the sides of the small triangles, cut 12 pieces of thick card, each 120 x 35mm (4¾ x 1¼in). Chamfer the 35mm (1¼in) ends of each piece, on the same face, so that a set

of three will fit neatly together when arranged as a triangle. Draw a line approximately 2.5mm (⅛in) from each end and chamfer by holding the knife at an angle and cutting along the edge of the card. (*See* Chapter 2, page 11.)

Cut nine pieces of the lining fabric and three of the outer covering fabric, approximately 10–15mm (½–¾in) larger all round than the card to be covered. If you are using a patterned fabric for the outer covering take the pattern into consideration when cutting the fabric in order to make the best use of the design.

Cover and lace the card pieces with the selected fabrics, so that the chamfered edges are on the unlaced side. Using strong thread, lace the short sides, mitre the corners, then lace the fabric across the longer pair of sides. (*See* Chapter 2, pages 12 and 13, for instructions.)

Place the covered cards in threes to form triangles, laced sides out, and ladder stitch or oversew the edges together.

Base

Measure the internal dimensions of these triangles and cut out four triangles, in thick card, for the bases.

Lace the bases with fabric to contrast with the sides of the triangles – three in the lining material and one in main fabric. Cut away excess fabric at the points of the triangle to make lacing easier.

Insert these triangles, laced side down, and stitch into place on the underside to lie flush with the sides, using ladder stitch and a curved needle.

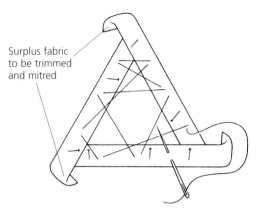

Fig 17.2 **Lacing fabric over a triangular piece of card.**

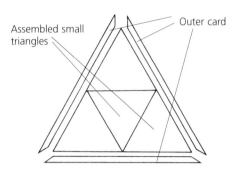

Fig 17.4 **Finding the dimensions for the outer sides.**

Assembly

Join all four completed triangular boxes together, along the top and bottom edges, using ladder stitch and a curved needle, to form one large triangular shape.

 If you have opted to make one large triangular lid for the box, allow for the edges to extend upwards slightly as well, so that the lining of the lid can fit inside this.

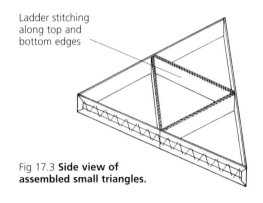

Fig 17.3 **Side view of assembled small triangles.**

Large triangle

Sides

Measure for the outer sides of the large triangle, allowing for a base card thickness and sufficient overlap at the points for the edges to be chamfered and joined. (*See* Figs 17.3 and 17.4.)

Chamfer the short edges of these card pieces, then cover and lace with outer fabric, this time lacing on the chamfered face. Ladder stitch or neatly oversew the short edges together, laced sides in, to form a large triangle.

Place the four small triangular boxes inside the large one, making sure that the top edges are flush. Stitch the top edges together, using ladder stitch and a curved needle.

Base

Measure the underside of the large triangle to obtain the dimensions for the large triangular base, to be cut in thick card, allowing for the fabric covering.

Cover and lace the base with lining or outer fabric (according to personal choice) and stitch into position, laced surface inside, using ladder stitch and a curved needle.

Lids

Separate lids can be made for each of the small boxes or one large lid made for the whole box. Whichever you choose, the lids are effectively flush flat lids as described in Chapter 3 (*see* pages 17 and 18).

Small lids

Measure the external dimensions of the smaller triangular boxes and cut out four triangles, in thick card, accordingly. Next, measure the internal dimensions and cut out triangles to fit, in thin card.

Measure and mark the centres of the thick card triangles as shown in Fig 17.6 and make a hole or holes, as appropriate, for the chosen lid 'knob'.

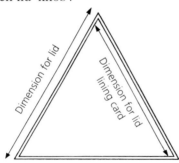

Fig 17.5 **Finding the dimensions for the lids and linings for the small triangular boxes.**

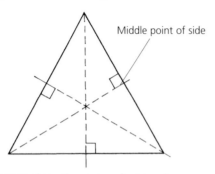

Fig 17.6 **Marking the centre of a triangle.**

If you wish to decorate the fabric for the lids, this should be worked now.

For each lid, use fabric to contrast with the base of the small triangular box it will cover. Pad, if required, and lace the fabric over the thick card, keeping the lacing well in from the edge of the card to avoid any stitches showing when the lining is in place.

Position a suitable button, bead, bow or other object in the centre of each lid and secure in place by passing a strong thread through the card and fastening it off securely on the underside.

Lace the thin card triangles with the appropriate contrasting fabric and ladder stitch each one to the underside of a lid, laced sides facing, using ladder stitch and a curved needle.

Large lid

The dimensions of the thin card lining will be the same as those for the base of the box. Cover and lace this card with lining fabric.

Measure the overall dimensions of the box top and cut out this large triangle in thick card. Mark the centre (*see* Fig 17.6).

Cut a piece of the outer covering fabric for this card, decorate, if required, and lace it over the card. Fasten your chosen lid knob in the centre, through the card, fastening it off securely on the underside.

Attach the lid lining card to the underside of the lid, along the outer edges of the lining, using ladder stitch and a curved needle.

Chapter Eighteen
Chest of drawers

This chest of drawers will prove useful in many locations, for the storage of jewellery, needlework threads and equipment or knick-knacks.

The fabrics now available are so attractive and varied that the box can be made up simply to show off the beauty of their patterns and designs. Alternatively, choose embroidery thread colours, a patchwork design or other needlecraft technique for the top of the box, to tone or contrast with the box itself, using plain or patterned fabrics.

For the box shown, I used patterned fabric for the drawer outers and the outer casing with a plain fabric for the drawer linings and, as a contrast, for the drawer casings.

Materials

Thick card, for carcass
Fabric A,
for drawers and outer casing:
approx. ¼m (¼yd)
Fabric B,
for drawer linings and casings:
approx. ¼m (¼yd)
Strong thread, for lacing
Threads to match both fabrics,
for sewing

Additional items
Curved needle

Cutting list (for each drawer)

Thick card	
Base (cut 2)	140 x 140mm (5½ x 5½in)
Side panels (cut 2)	140 x 40mm (5½ x 1½in)
Drawer front and back (cut 2)	145 x 40mm (5¾ x 1½in)

NB: It is very important that all measurements are precise and that the card is cut accurately.

Method

The most straightforward way to construct a chest of drawers is to build it up by starting with the construction of the drawers, then the drawer casings and finally the outer casing forming the actual box. It is, therefore, important to decide on the overall maximum dimensions of the box in the design stage and work backwards with the approximate calculations, to establish the size of the drawers.

Several drawers can be incorporated into a 'chest', including both long and short drawers: this particular design incorporates two short drawers.

In taking measurements and cutting card, always make allowances for the thickness of the fabric, turnings and lacings.

Drawer sides and base

For the first drawer, cut all the pieces listed in the cutting list. The front and back should lie across the sides to provide a smooth, unbroken drawer front. (*See* Fig 18.1.)

Cut the fabric you have chosen for the outside of the drawers (Fabric A) to cover the sides, back, base and front, allowing 20mm (¾in) turnings all round. Lace these over the card.

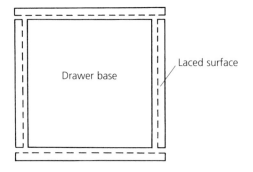

Fig 18.1 **Plan view of drawer base.**

The method to be used for opening the drawers should be decided upon now, before the front is attached to the drawer. Either a pull tab or a knob can be used.

Drawer Openings

Pull tab

To construct a pull tab, make a narrow tube of fabric or ribbon and stitch this to the centre of one of the laced sides of the covered base: it will then be sandwiched between the base and the front when the front is stitched into position (*see* Fig 18.2).

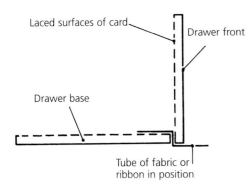

Laced surfaces of card

Drawer front

Drawer base

Tube of fabric or ribbon in position

Fig 18.2 **Positioning the fabric pull tab.**

Drawer knob

Alternatively, for a knob, stitch a button or similar through the drawer front, so that any fastening is on the back, where it will subsequently be hidden by the drawer lining.

To use a button with a shank as a drawer pull, mark the position of the button or buttons on the front of the drawer. Make a hole to take the shank through the fabric

and card, using a bradawl or other spike, from front to back. There will be a rough edge to the hole, so remove the surplus card from the back by trimming it away and smoothing the edges with sandpaper.

Push the shank through the hole and thread a short length of thin, stiff wire through the shank, thus holding the button in place. Place masking tape over the wire to fix it in position.

Drawer assembly

Attach the covered sides, laced sides in, to the covered base, laced side up, using a matching sewing thread and ladder stitch with a curved needle. Stitch the front and back panels into place in the same way.

Lining

Measure the internal dimensions of the drawer, including the height, and, allowing for the fabric covering, cut card as indicated in Fig 18.3 so that the covered side, front and back cards will be flush with the top of the drawer when stitched into position.

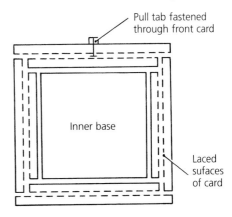

Pull tab fastened through front card

Inner base

Laced sufaces of card

Fig 18.3 **Plan view of drawer showing inner base.**

Cut lining fabric (Fabric B) for each of the resulting pieces of card and lace. Stitch each side into position inside the drawer carcass along the top edges, laced surfaces together, using a curved needle. Measure for and cut card for the inner base, then lace with lining fabric so that it will push-fit into place. If required, the card surfaces of the outer and inner bases can be lightly glued and pressed together to hold the inner base in position.

Repeat the process, using the same dimensions, for the second drawer.

Drawer casings

Measure the outer dimensions of each drawer and cut card according to Fig 18.4, allowing for the fabric covering and remembering that the drawer will need to slide in and out from the casing.

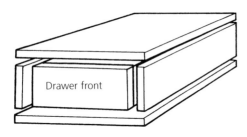

Fig 18.4 **Assembly of card for outer casing.**

When calculating the length of the casing sides, add one thickness of card to the length of the drawer to allow for a piece of covered card to be inserted at the back of the casing (see the Chest of Drawers in Chapter 13, pages 67 and 68).

Cut card for the casings of both drawers at the same time as they will be identical.

Lace Fabric B over the pieces of card and ladder stitch the pieces for each casing together, laced surfaces out.

With the drawer in position to stabilize the casing, measure for the back panel insert, allowing for the fabric covering. Cut the card, lace it with fabric and position it flush with the back of the casing, laced surface out. Ladder stitch the panel into place using a curved needle.

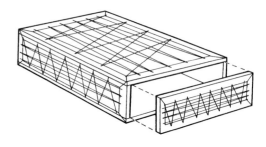

Fig 18.5 **Inserting the back panel into the casing.**

Once the drawers and their casings have been assembled, ladder stitch the casings securely together.

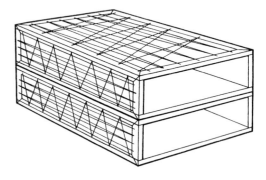

Fig 18.6 **The casings ready to be stitched together.**

Outer casing

Take measurements as for the drawer casings, including allowing for the fabric covering and the insertion of a back panel. Cut the appropriate card pieces, lace with Fabric A and stitch them together, laced surfaces in. Position the drawer casings inside this outer casing and stitch them into position.

Platform base

Cut a piece of card 10mm (½in) larger all round than the outer casing and cover this with Fabric A, keeping the lacing stitches well in from the edges so that they will not show when the casing is in position.

Place the outer casing centrally on this base, pin securely, and stitch it into position using ladder stitch and a curved needle.

Top

Cut a piece of card the same size as the platform base, mount any embroidery, patchwork or other decoration, or simply pad it and lace with Fabric A.

Placing the completed top upside down on a soft surface such as felt or towelling (in order to avoid crushing any decoration), turn the chest of drawers upside down and position it centrally on the top. Stitch into position with a curved needle.

Chapter Nineteen
Octagonal box with drawers

This is a perfect design for keeping sewing equipment tidily and accessibly – in a most beautiful and decorative box. Select a patterned fabric for the outside of the box, possibly to co-ordinate with room furnishings, and choose a plain, contrasting fabric for the drawer casings and linings which will serve to set off the detail.

Unlike the Chest of Drawers in Chapter 18, this design starts from a base of fixed dimensions, so in this case it is necessary to construct the drawer casings, to fit the base, before constructing the drawers.

Decide on the size of the box, according

Materials

Thick card, for carcass
Thin card, for lining
Lining fabric
Outer covering fabric
Strong thread, for lacing
Thread to match covering fabric or
lining, for sewing
Drawer pulls or tabs as required
(buttons, ribbons, etc.)

Additional items
Curved needle

to its probable location and the amount of storage space required, and on the toning fabrics to be used. The box illustrated required a 150mm (6in) radius for the basic octagon – giving an overall width dimension of more than 300mm (12in) – and the drawer casings are 40mm (1½in).

Method

Lower Layer

Top and base
Using the radius chosen, draw two circles, then mark and cut out two octagons in thick card. (*See* Octagonal Box, page 52, for instructions on constructing octagons.)

Lace both card pieces with the outer fabric. One of these will be the base and the other the top of the drawer section of the box: the top will also be the base of the upper layer box.

Drawer casings
Cut casings for the long drawers by carefully measuring across the base, remembering to allow for the thickness of the fabric.

Cut and lace the plain fabric firmly over the casing pieces.

Assemble the basic casings then measure, cut, lace and fit each with a back panel (*see* Drawer casings, Chapter 13, page 67). Stitch the two casings together, back to back, using ladder stitch and a curved needle.

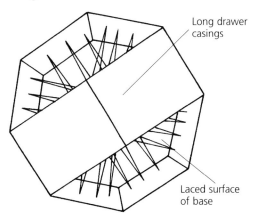

Fig 19.1 **The long drawer casings.**

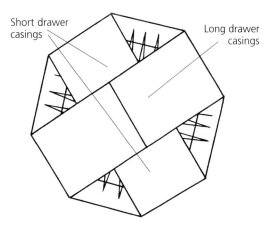

Fig 19.2 **Positioning the short drawer casings.**

89

Pin these casings into position on the box base and measure for the short drawer casings, which will be set at right angles to the long drawers, again allowing for fabric in your measurements.

Assemble these short drawer casings, then join them to the long drawer casings, positioning them carefully to align with the sides of the base (*see* Fig 19.2).

Drawers

Measure the casings to find the dimensions for the drawers to fit them: each pair should be identical if the casings have been accurately cut and assembled. Cut and cover the card pieces for the drawers, using the patterned fabric for the outer covering and the plain fabric for the lining. Assemble the drawers as shown on pages 84–86, in Chapter 13.

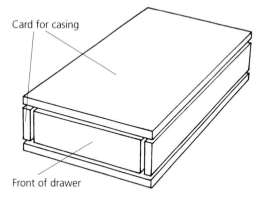

Card for casing

Front of drawer

Fig 19.3 **Casing with drawer in position.**

Assembly

Attach the drawer casings to the base card, laced side up, stitching firmly. Place the second covered octagon, laced side down, on top of the casings and attach it to the casings, once again using ladder stitch and a curved needle.

Carefully measure the spaces between the casings and cut card to fit, allowing for the fabric covering. Chamfer the edges of these card pieces so that they fit closely between the casings. (*See* Chapter 2, page 11.)

Cut pieces of outer fabric to lace over the chamfered card (lacing on the chamfered surface) and stitch into position using ladder stitch and a curved needle.

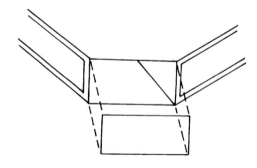

Fig 19.4 **Card cut to fit the spaces between the casings.**

Upper Layer

Sides

For the outside pieces of the upper layer box, measure the edges of the octagon and cut eight identical pieces of card using this measurement for the length of the card and the required height of the box for the width.

Lace these pieces with outer fabric and ladder stitch them all together in a row to form the outside of the upper layer of the box.

Position the pieces around the circumference of the octagon, laced surfaces inside, and stitch them into position using ladder stitch and a curved needle. Stitch the edges of the two free sides together to finish.

Lining

Measure and cut eight pieces of thin card to line the sides of the octagonal box. Lace these with the plain fabric and ladder stitch together in a row, laced side outwards.

 If divisions are required in this upper layer of the box, measure and fit them at this stage, prior to stitching the lining into the box. (*See* Chapter 5.)

Position the lining unit inside the box and stitch it to the outer sides along the top edge, using ladder stitch and a curved needle.

 If a hinged lid is required, fit the hinge whilst stitching the lining unit into place. (*See* Chapter 9, pages 40 and 41.)

Lid

Mark out and cut card for the lid, using a slightly larger radius, and decorate the fabric as desired before assembling the lid unit. Line the lid as required and attach it to the hinge if a hinge is fitted.

This box could also be mounted on a platform base. Cut such a base to the same dimensions as the lid.

Chapter Twenty
Three-tier box

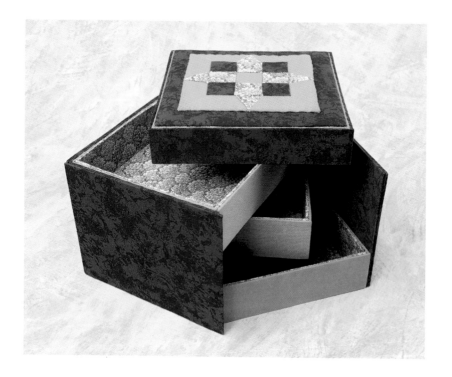

This innovative design provides plenty of storage space for items connected with any hobby, particularly such things as embroidery threads, needles and scissors. It enables items to be kept conveniently together but separated.

The basic concept is that two or three trays are suspended by strong paper fasteners to different sides of an outer box in such a way that the layers swing out as the box is opened. Using three contrasting or toning fabrics makes this a very attractive as well as functional box.

The instructions given refer to a three-tier box but could equally be applied to a box with just two tiers.

Method

The Trays
Start by constructing the three trays, making them identical in size. Use one

Materials

Thick card, for carcass
Thin card, for lining
Co-ordinating fabrics x 3:
½m (½yd) of each
Paper binders x 12
Washers x 12
Strong thread, for lacing
Thread to match covering fabric
or lining, for sewing

Additional items
Curved needle

Cutting list (for each tray)

Thick card

Outer base (cut 1)	180 x 180mm (7 x 7 in)
Outer sides (cut 2)	182 x 50mm (7⅛ x 2in)
Outer back (cut 1)	180 x 50mm (7 x 2in)
Outer front (cut 1)	184 x 50mm (7¼ x 2in)

NB: It is very important that all measurements are precise and that the card is cut accurately.

fabric for the outside and a contrasting fabric for the linings. The dimensions given here are for the box shown.

For each tray, cut all the card pieces listed in the cutting list. The front and back should lie across the shorter sides to provide smooth, unbroken ends to the tray.

Cut pieces from the fabric you have chosen for the outer case of the trays to cover the sides, back, base and front pieces, allowing 20mm (¾in) turnings all round,

and lace these over the card pieces.

Attach the covered sides, laced sides in, to the covered base, laced side up, then stitch the front and back panels into place.

Lining

Measure the internal dimensions of the tray, including the height, and cut the appropriate pieces of card, remembering to allow for the fabric covering. The covered lining pieces should be flush with the top of the tray when stitched into position.

Cut contrasting fabric to cover the resulting pieces of card and lace the fabric over the card.

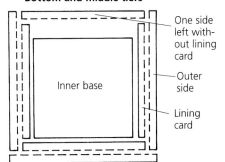

Fig 20.1 **Positioning the linings in each tray prior to attaching the fasteners.**

Insert the pieces of lining card as shown in Fig 20.1 so that for the bottom and middle tray, one long and two short sides are in place while for the top tray, just one long and one short side are in place. Ladder stitch them into place along the top edge.

Attaching the fasteners

To establish the points at which the trays are to be fastened to the sides of the main box, mark the central point and the mid-points between this point and either side, on the sides of the trays with no lining pieces attached. On the top tray, there will be two sides with this set of points marked.

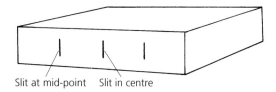

Slit at mid-point   Slit in centre

Fig 20.2 **Marking the points for the fasteners on the tray.**

Using the point of a Stanley or craft knife, make small slits through the fabric and card at each of the points marked, and pass a strong paper fastener through each slit from the inside of the tray to the outside.

Fig 20.3 **The paper fasteners inserted through the side of the tray.**

Position the remaining lining pieces in the trays – these will cover the heads of the paper fasteners – and stitch them into

position along the top edges, using ladder stitch and a curved needle.

The Main Box

Inner sides

Place the trays on top of one another and, referring to Fig 20.7, measure to find the dimensions for the inner sides of the main box. Cut four pieces of thick card to size. Mark the side pieces where slits are required to receive the paper fasteners from the trays.

To find the points accurately, rule horizontal lines, in pencil, to divide each side into three. These lines will indicate the level of each tier. One side will then need slits in the bottom third, one side will need slits in the middle third and two sides will need slits in the top third.

Find the points for these slits by marking the central point in the appropriate third, and the mid-points between this and either side, both horizontally and vertically. With a Stanley or craft knife, make slits in the card at the points where these horizontal and vertical lines cross.

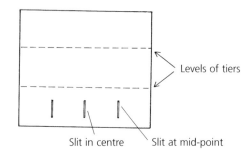

Levels of tiers

Slit in centre   Slit at mid-point

Fig 20.4 **Marking the points on the side pieces to take the fasteners from the bottom tray.**

Cut out the chosen fabric and lace it over the side pieces, making sure that the marks for the slits are on the laced surface. Make small slits through the card and fabric to allow for a paper fastener to be passed through from the unlaced side.

Assembly

Using ladder stitch and a curved needle, attach each tray to its side piece along each edge. Join the side pieces together, stitching on the outside.

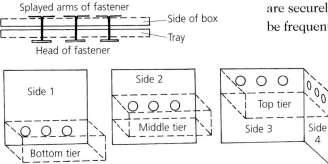

Fig 20.5 **Attaching the trays to the side pieces.**

Using a length of outer fabric, doubled and stitched so that the resulting piece is just shorter than the height of the box, stitch this around the back corner of the box, on the laced sides, as shown in Fig 20.6, thus providing a hinge on which the box will swivel.

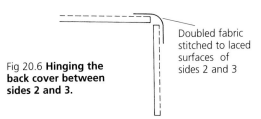

Fig 20.6 **Hinging the back cover between sides 2 and 3.**

Outer sides

Again, referring to Fig 20.7, take measurements from the assembly so far to find the dimensions for the outer sides of the box, remembering to take into consideration the thickness of the card and covering fabric. You will find that the dimensions of these outer sides vary.

Cut out the outer sides in thick card and lace them with the appropriate fabric. Attach these to the inner sides, laced sides together, along each edge, using ladder stitch and a curved needle. Ensure that the leading edges are securely and neatly finished as these will be frequently handled.

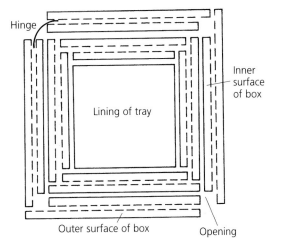

Fig 20.7 **Plan view of card arrangement for three-tier box.**

Lid

Contrary to the usual procedure, the lining for the lid will have to be made before the lid itself. Since this measurement is dependent on the box which has been constructed, the outer pieces of the lid will be constructed after the lining.

Lining

Close the tiered box and measure for the lip linings. Decide on the depth of the lip for the lid. Cut the lining pieces for the lip in thick card (in order to give the lid greater stability in construction), and lace them with the appropriate fabric. Stitch the pieces together, laced surfaces outside, following the arrangement shown in Fig 20.8.

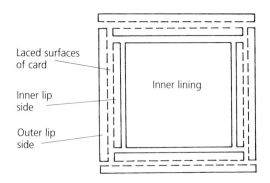

Laced surfaces of card

Inner lip side

Outer lip side

Inner lining

Fig 20.8 **Plan view of card arrangement for lid lip side linings, outer sides and inner lining.**

Outer sides

Measure and cut thick card pieces for the outer sides of the lip and lace them with the chosen fabric. With the laced surfaces of the outer and inner cards facing and placed in the correct order, ladder stitch them together using a curved needle, on all edges.

To find the dimensions for the top of the lid illustrated, take measurements across the inside of the lid lip. Alternatively, the top of the lid can lie right across the lip, in which case measure across the outside of the lip. Cut the thick card accordingly, then cut a piece of thin card for the lining, remembering to allow for the fabric covering.

 If the lid fabric is to be embellished, this should be worked now.

Assembly

Cover both pieces of card with the appropriate fabric. Using a curved needle, ladder stitch the thick card piece into position on all sides, laced side down. Glue the laced surface of the lining card lightly and position it inside the lid, with the laced sides of both lid pieces facing. Leave to dry under pressure.

Chapter Twenty-one
Victorian-style étui

This fascinating box is a real 'conversation piece' since it always arouses such interest when the lid is removed to reveal the unusual interior, which collapses outwards to show off the contents. Etui is a French word meaning case or cover, in this context for needlework tools.

The card required for this style of box is less substantial than the greyboard employed for other fabric-covered boxes, since étui are much smaller and more delicate. However, a strong, firm card is required – mounting board is ideal. The thin card required for the linings can be cut from cereal packaging or similar.

Method

Cutting and covering the card

Cut all the pieces listed in the cutting list. Referring to Fig 21.1, cover pieces A, B, C, D and E with the outer fabric, using fine nylon or strong polyester thread for lacing. An ideal fabric for the outer covering of an étui is a fine cotton with a small design or stripes, or plain if any decoration is planned. The lining should also be a fine cotton to tone with the outer fabric. Mitre all the corners and ensure that they lie flat; stitch down neatly if necessary.

Pad pieces I and J with thin felt or polyester wadding before covering them with the chosen lining fabric; lace securely and mitre all the corners, ensuring that they lie flat.

Cutting list

Mounting board

A	Platform base (cut 1)	98 x 98mm (4 x 4in)
B	Outer box base (cut 1)	87 x 87mm (3½ x 3½in)
C	Inner box base (cut 1)	40 x 40mm (1½ x 1½in)
D	Outer box sides (cut 4)	104 x 87mm (4⅛ x 3½in)
E	Inner box sides (cut 4)	80 x 40mm (3⅛ x 1½in)
F	Central box sides (cut 1; to be scored)	80 x 50mm (3 x 2in)
G	Lid drops (cut 4)	92 x 15mm (3¾ x ⅝in)

Thin card

I	Outer box (cut 4)	82 x 99mm (3¼ x 3⅞in)
J	Inner box (cut 4)	75 x 35mm (2⅞ x 1¼in)

NB: It is very important that all measurements are precise and that the card is cut accurately.

With the exception of the inserts for the lid (labelled H in the diagram), the pieces of card used to construct an étui can all be cut out at the same time.

Assembling the outer box

For the outer box, line up one side piece (D) with the base (B), placing the right side of B and the wrong side of D together. (*See* Chapter 2, page 14.) Stitch these together and attach the other three sides to the base in the same way.

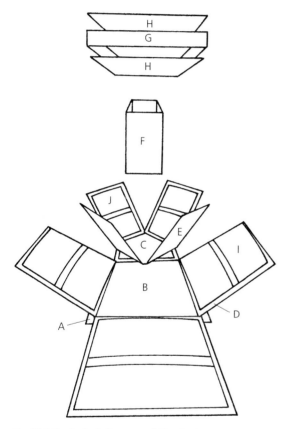

Fig 21.1 **Exploded diagram of the étui.**

Position the ribbons around the linings (I) and stitch them into place on the backs. Centre each lining piece (I) on its corresponding fabric-covered side, laced surfaces together, and ladder stitch firmly

into place, using a curved needle, catching the ribbons at the same time.

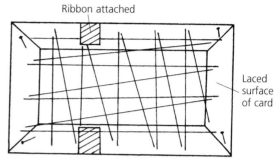

Fig 21.2 **Attaching the ribbon to the back of the lining.**

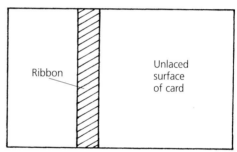

Fig 21.3 **The ribbon positioned on the front of the lining.**

Inner box

Repeat the procedure as for the outer box using base C, sides E and lining pieces J. When complete, lightly glue the underside of the inner box in the very middle and position it diagonally inside the outer box, pressing it firmly onto base B. (*See* Fig 21.4 for the angle of positioning.)

Leave to dry overnight under pressure and then ladder stitch into position all round using a curved needle.

Place the platform base (A) laced side uppermost on a flat surface and position the outer box centrally on this base. Stitch them firmly together around the edge, using ladder stitch with a curved needle. Keep the sides of the box upright by holding them with an elastic band or string to make this procedure easier.

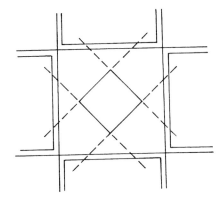

Fig 21.4 **Positioning the middle box.**

Lid

Lay the sides of the lid (G) in a line on the outer covering fabric. Cut a piece of the fabric twice the depth of the card plus a little extra for the seam allowance. Fold the edges in and pin the fabric tightly against the card. Stitch the seam either by hand, using back stitch, or with the zip foot of a machine. After stitching, pull the fabric round the card until the seam is far enough up inside to allow for the covered lid card to be inserted and lie flush with the edges of the sides. (See Figs 7.4–7.7, page 30.) Stitch across the two ends of the side pieces and then ladder stitch the two ends together.

Measure accurately to find the dimensions required for the lid top insert and lining so that these will fit snugly when covered with fabric. Cut the top piece from mounting board and the lining from thin card.

Pad, cover and decorate the card for the top of the box as required, then stitch firmly into place to lie flush with the top edge of the lid sides. Cover the lid lining card with lining fabric and glue it lightly inside the lid, card to card.

If a 'domed' effect is required, cut three squares of padding, one the size of the lid, the second slightly smaller, and the third slightly smaller again. Arrange these pieces on the fabric as shown in Fig 21.5, position the card and lace the fabric over it.

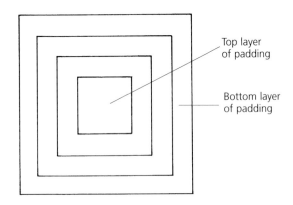

Top layer of padding

Bottom layer of padding

Fig 21.5 **Arrangement of lid padding to give a domed effect.**

The lid holds the sides of the outer box in a closed position. It can be hinged if required, by applying one end of a doubled strip of the outer covering fabric to one of the sides of the outer box (matching the pattern carefully to avoid this showing too clearly) and stitching the other end to the inside of the finished lid (see Fig 21.6).

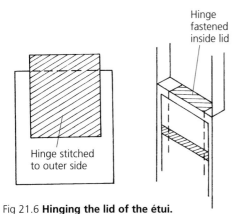

Hinge
fastened
inside lid

Hinge stitched
to outer side

Fig 21.6 **Hinging the lid of the étui.**

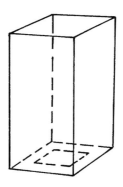

Fig 21.8 **The scored card folded into shape.**

Central box

Score across the central box card (F) at 20mm (¾in) intervals. Completely cover this card with fabric as for the lid sides, moving the fabric around the card in the same way. Bend the covered card along the scored lines to form a four-sided box, seam on the inside, and ladder stitch the two joining sides together.

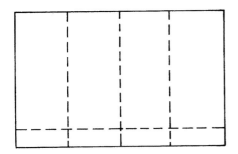

Fig 21.7 **Scoring the card to make up the central box.**

Cut a small square of card to fit inside the central box, lace it with fabric and ladder stitch it into place to give the box rigidity. Position the central box in the centre of the inner box, with its sides at right angles to those of the inner box and parallel to the outer box. Fix in place with a little glue and leave to dry under pressure. Ladder stitch all round using a curved needle.

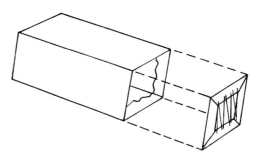

Fig 21.9 **Inserting the base into the central box.**

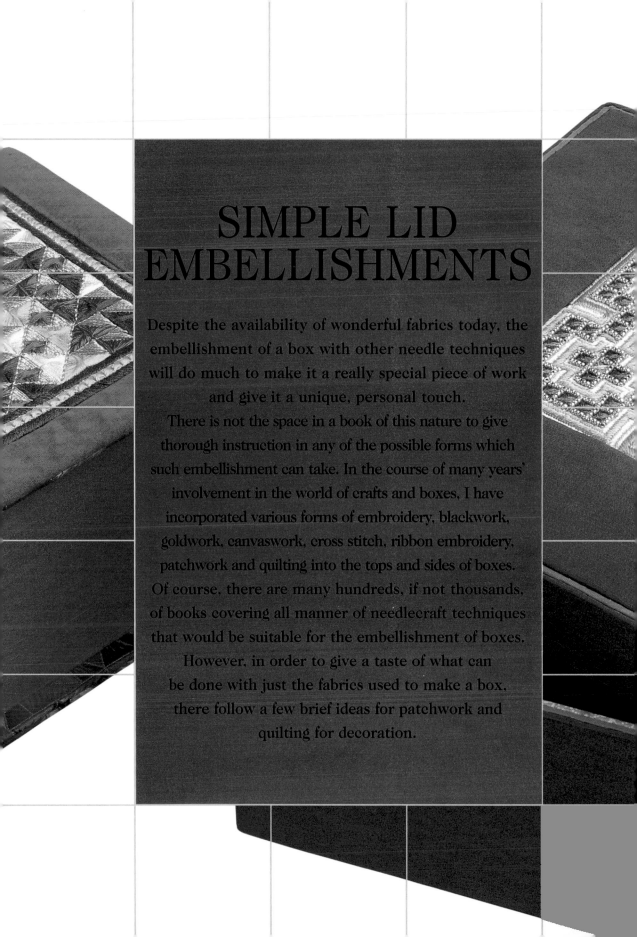

SIMPLE LID EMBELLISHMENTS

Despite the availability of wonderful fabrics today, the embellishment of a box with other needle techniques will do much to make it a really special piece of work and give it a unique, personal touch.

There is not the space in a book of this nature to give thorough instruction in any of the possible forms which such embellishment can take. In the course of many years' involvement in the world of crafts and boxes, I have incorporated various forms of embroidery, blackwork, goldwork, canvaswork, cross stitch, ribbon embroidery, patchwork and quilting into the tops and sides of boxes. Of course, there are many hundreds, if not thousands, of books covering all manner of needlecraft techniques that would be suitable for the embellishment of boxes.

However, in order to give a taste of what can be done with just the fabrics used to make a box, there follow a few brief ideas for patchwork and quilting for decoration.

Chapter Twenty-two
Patchwork

There are many and various patchwork techniques, even the simplest of which makes an effective decoration for boxes: and patchwork has the virtue of using up scraps of the fabric from which the box itself has been made.

Only three ideas are suggested here but if you would like more detailed information, there are many books available on the numerous techniques which have evolved and which are still being developed.

Hexagonal patchwork

This simple, repeating shape is an easy one for a beginner and through the careful use of colour and arrangement of shapes, very satisfactory results can be obtained. The patchwork can then be stitched to the lids or sides of boxes. Plan your design to establish the number of hexagons required and the fabrics to be used.

Decide what size you require for the basic hexagon. This should be in scale with the final size required – the smaller the design, the smaller the hexagon.

Cut out the required hexagon in thick card to form a template. (If suitable, this can be photocopied or traced from Fig 22.2.) Use this thick card template to draw

hexagons onto very thin card (old birthday card backs prove ideal for this purpose) or even thick paper, and cut out a sufficient number to complete the design.

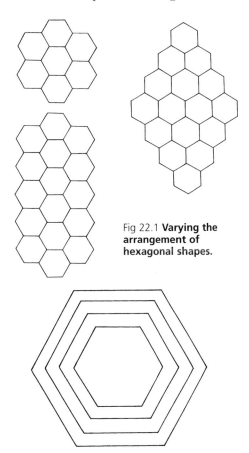

Fig 22.1 **Varying the arrangement of hexagonal shapes.**

Fig 22.2 **Specimen hexagonal templates.**

Fig 22.3 **Tacking the paper linings into place.**

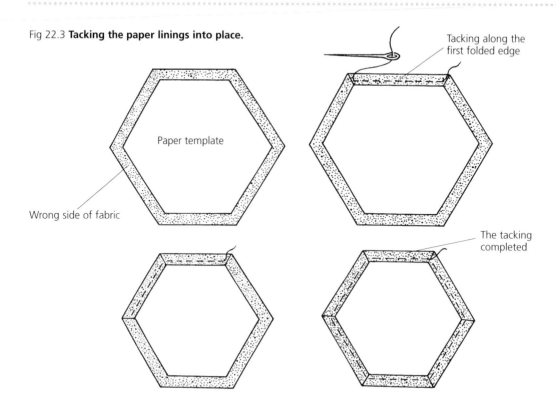

Paper template

Wrong side of fabric

Tacking along the
first folded edge

The tacking
completed

Do the same to cut out hexagonal fabric shapes, adding a seam allowance of 6mm (¼in) all round. Pin each hexagonal paper template in the centre of the fabric shape, on the wrong side. Fold the seam allowance tightly over the paper along one edge and tack: start with a knot to make removing the tacking easier at the end. Fold over the second side, tack into place, and continue round the hexagon until all six sides have been tacked.

Placing the patches in order, right sides facing, join them together by oversewing along each edge, using a fine needle and matching thread. When all the patches have been joined, remove the paper linings.

Apply the patchwork to the fabric pieces for the box by ladder stitching all round, using a curved needle. This can even be done after a box has been completed and looks well applied to a padded surface.

If you have enjoyed using this hexagonal shape as a first patchwork experience, there are many other shapes which can be used in a similar way, for example, diamonds, triangles, octagons, pentagons, rhomboids, trapezoids, etc. Metal and plastic templates can be purchased for many of these, in sets, and different shapes can be combined. The possibilities for designs are endless.

Three-shapes cross patchwork

Fig 22.4 **A three-shapes cross design.**

This slightly different technique involves three templates: rather than cut out paper linings, the templates are used to draw directly onto the wrong side of the fabrics. Three contrasting fabrics are required.

The design relies on the finished shape

Cutting list

Fabric A

Template 1	(cut 4 with the template one way up and 4 with it reversed)
Template 2	(cut 1)

Fabric B

Template 2	(cut 4)

Fabric C

Template 2	(cut 4)
Template 3	(cut 4)

being a square and it makes life easier if the measurements of the sides are easily divisible by five! Draw your square, to the size required, on paper and divide it in accordance with Fig 22.5.

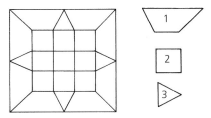

Fig 22.5 **The finished block for the three-shapes cross patchwork and the resulting templates.**

Cut out the three shapes in thick card to use as templates. Draw around the templates in pencil onto the wrong side of the selected fabrics, cutting 6mm (¼in) away from the pencil line for each piece, to allow for the seams.

Place the fabric patches, right sides together, with the pencilled lines matching. These tracing lines are now the stitching lines: sew along the lines using small running stitches and finish each end off securely. (Sew only on the lines and not through the seam allowance.)

The simplest method of assembly is to stitch the central squares into strips of three and join these to make the centre block, and then to sew the patches for each of the four sides together in strips. Attach each side strip to the centre square and then sew along the corners.

Press the block carefully and apply the finished patchwork to the padded lid by stitching all round using ladder stitch with a curved needle.

Folded star patchwork

This technique, which is sometimes referred to as Somerset patchwork, involves folding small rectangles of fabric into triangles and stitching these onto a backing square in a series of concentric circles.

Fig 22.6 **An example of folded star patchwork.**

Start by cutting a square of cotton backing fabric a little larger than the size of the finished circle required, find the centre and divide the square into eight, marking the lines with a pencil (*See* Fig 22.7.)

Plan the layout of your chosen fabrics, bearing in mind the number of rounds needed and the finished result. The patchwork on the box shown here involved three rounds of triangles, with the diameter of the finished circle being 90mm (3½in).

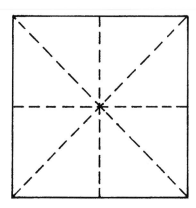

Fig 22.7 **Marking the backing fabric for the folded star patchwork.**

Cut rectangles of fabric measuring 60 x 36mm (2¼ x 1½in). You will need four for the first round, eight for the second round and eight for the third round. (Any additional rounds would require more rectangles: fourth, fifth and sixth rounds would each require 16 rectangles, the seventh, eighth and ninth 32 rectangles, and so on.)

For each rectangle, fold the long side down 6mm (¼in), then fold in the corners to make a triangle, as shown in Fig 22.8. Ensure that the folds are very precise and that the edges meet centrally. Press all the triangles.

Position the first triangle at the centre of the backing fabric and secure the point to the backing with a tiny stitch (*see* Fig 22.9). Tack across the base of the triangle, trimming the corners away to avoid excess bulk.

Repeat this with the other three triangles to complete the first round, making sure that their points and edges meet exactly – there should not be any backing fabric showing.

For the second round use a contrasting fabric. Position each triangle on one of the

Fig 22.8 **Folding the fabric rectangles to form triangles.**

The fabric rectangle

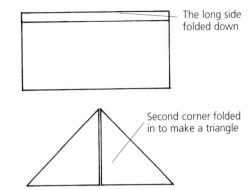

The long side folded down

First corner folded in

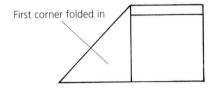

Second corner folded in to make a triangle

radiating lines on the backing square, placing each point at the same distance from the centre and lining them all up with care. Fix each point with a tiny stitch and tack along the bottom of each triangle as before, trimming away the corner excess.

For the third and any subsequent rounds, position the point of each fresh triangle at the same distance from the centre, stitching and tacking as before. When the circle is sufficiently large for the purpose, mount and present as required.

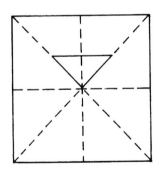

Fig 22.9 **Positioning the first triangle.**

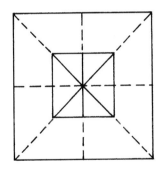

Fig 22.10 **The first round of triangles.**

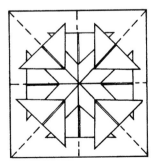

Fig 22.11 **The second round of triangles.**

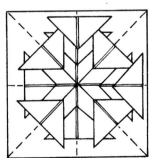

Fig 22.12 **Positioning the third round of triangles.**

Chapter Twenty-three
Quilting

Fig 23.1 **An example of decorative quilting.**

The lid of a box may be simply enhanced by quilting the fabric where the design allows for stitching around the outlines of flowers, leaves, etc. To quilt a printed fabric design, follow the basic procedure given below.

Choose the area of the fabric to be quilted and cut one, two or three layers of wadding as required (bear in mind that this will squash down considerably when quilting), a minimum of 25mm (1in) larger all round than the area to be quilted.

Cut a piece of lining fabric to the same dimensions as the main fabric, which should be 50mm (2in) bigger all round than the area to be quilted. Sandwich the wadding layers between the two fabrics and pin together in several places, keeping the whole as flat as possible.

Starting with the centre lines, tack lines

Materials

Fabric, for quilting
Lining fabric, thin cotton or similar
Thin wadding
Frame, at least 25mm (1in) larger
all round than the design chosen
Tacking cotton
Usual sewing equipment
Drawing pins
Quilting thread, to match or contrast
with the fabric design outline

at 25mm (1in) intervals, through all the layers, gradually working outwards until the entire fabric is covered by a grid of tacked lines holding the layers together, as shown in Figs 23.2–23.4.

Mount the tacked fabrics onto the frame, using drawing pins or staples. Fix the first drawing pins at the centre of each side and work outwards on alternate sides, keeping the fabric square and taut as you work.

Quilt the design using a 'run and back stitch' technique, following the chosen lines of the design. Use a suitable quilting thread,

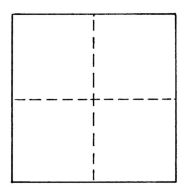

Fig 23.2 **The central lines tacked into position.**

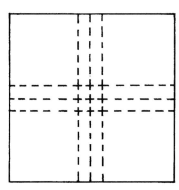

Fig 23.3 **The next four lines tacked in place.**

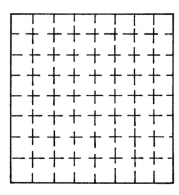

Fig 23.4 **The surface of the fabric with the tacking completed.**

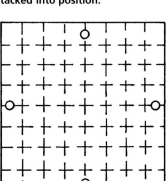

Fig 23.5 **The first four drawing pins in place.**

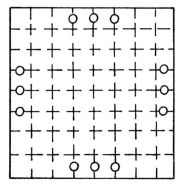

Fig 23.6 **Additional drawing pins inserted.**

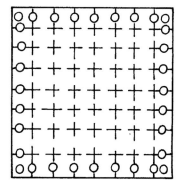

Fig 23.7 **The fabric ready for quilting.**

preferably chosen to match or tone with the line which the quilting is following, for example, a metallic gold thread would look good on a gold line.

Fig 23.8 **Quilting over the lines of the fabric design.**

When the quilting has been completed, take the fabric off the frame and remove the tacking stitches. The backing fabric and the wadding may need to be cut away from around the design, depending on the final use to which the quilted fabric will be put.

For a box lid

Trim both the wadding and the lining to the size of the lid, so that only the single thickness of the main fabric is laced over the card.

Follow the instructions given in Chapter 2 for lacing fabric over card (see page 12) and see Chapter 3 for constructing the lid according to the design chosen.

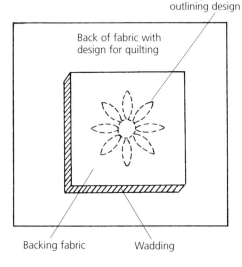

Quilting stitches outlining design

Back of fabric with design for quilting

Backing fabric

Wadding

Fig 23.9 **The back of the quilting, with the padding and the backing fabric trimmed.**

Chapter Twenty-four
Mounting in a frame

According to the needle technique that has been used in creating the embellishment for your box, follow any specific advice for stretching the work and/or any other preparation needed before mounting.

Lace the work tightly over a piece of mounting board, cut to the exact dimensions of the work, so that no surplus fabric is visible on the right side. Mitre the corners as neatly as possible, cutting away any excess to reduce bulk.

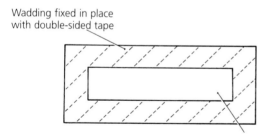

Wadding fixed in place with double-sided tape

Panel cut out for embroidery

Fig 24.1 **Positioning the wadding on the embroidery frame.**

Cut a panel from the centre of the lid card to the dimensions of the decorated panel, thus making a frame for the decoration. Next, cut a piece of thin wadding to the exact dimensions of the frame and position it carefully on the card with double-sided tape.

To cover the frame, cut a piece of firm, iron-on interfacing, 20mm (¾in) larger all round than the lid card, and iron the interfacing onto the wrong side of a piece of outer fabric cut to the same dimensions.

Position the padded frame face down on the interfacing. Draw the inner outline of the framework on the interfacing and carefully cut through the centre of the interfacing and fabric, as indicated in Fig 24.2, and into the corners. Place double-sided tape on the card frame and then, repositioning the fabric underneath, pull the fabric gently through the frame and fix it in position on the tape.

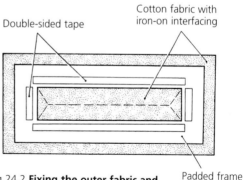

Double-sided tape

Cotton fabric with iron-on interfacing

Padded frame

Fig 24.2 **Fixing the outer fabric and interfacing in place over the frame.**

Insert the decorated panel into the frame and fix it firmly in place on the back with masking tape.

Finally, lace the outer fabric over the back of the card, and line the lid as required.

GALLERY

Bridge box

This box acted as a container for other craft items which constituted the entry of my Women's Institute at the time, in the Co-operative Craft Competition at another West Midlands Show – we came third. It is simply a large-scale rectangular box (I had a piece of hardboard cut for the base to make it stronger but laced this as usual) with a sliding tray. My intended final use for the box was for storing bridge items, with the quilted lid lining having a club, heart, diamond and spade cut out from the outer fabric and applied, with a gold thread couched around each one. The tablecloth lying on the tray is made from the same fabric as the box lining and has the suit symbols appliquéd in the corners.

Napkin box

I actually made this as the prototype for a box wanted by my friend and co-author Daphne Ashby (we wrote *Ribbon Embroidery* and *Creative Embroidery Techniques using Colour through Gold* together) as a presentation box to contain a beautiful piece of stumpwork she had worked. It is based on a chocolate box Daphne had seen and described to me. The result is used to store some paper napkins,

which have a similar grape design on them. It was necessary to start with the inner box, which I made using the double-layer method, then carefully measure and cut card for the linings of the two lifting sections, followed by their outer covering, including a hinge. The two lifting sections were then attached by their hinges underneath the main box. To finish, the main box was stitched to a platform base.

Hexagonal needlework box

Having seen someone using a box similar to this for needlework items, I decided to make one from the left-over fabric from the Napkin Box on page 114, centralizing a bunch of grapes on the loose lid. Using a hexagonal base, I cut card and laced the outer sides with fabric individually. I then attached these to the base and cut the card

for the lining pieces. I made the individual linings as shown and stitched each to its outer partner all round, using a curved needle. I joined three of the sides together but left the others to drop down. I made a simple lid and use a braid to hold the sides together but a lid with a lip would serve this purpose as well.

Chest of drawers with embroidered upstand

The embroidery on the upstand is the result of an experimental weekend with the South Cheshire Branch of the Embroiderers' Guild at Plas Tan-y-Bwlch. We used nylon tights, stretched on a round frame, and machine embroidery, sequin waste, hand embroidery, net, beads, etc., etc., to be 'creative' … but then what? So I made another box. Amongst my accumulated fabrics, I found some lovely flowered cotton material with all the colours of the embroidery. I used this to line the drawers of the chest and another green/gold fabric to cover it. The last element to be stitched into place was the shaped upstand with the embroidery.

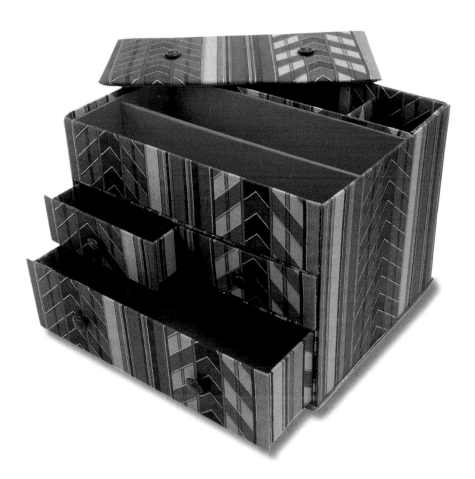

Calligraphy box

This large box is the result of coming across the striped fabric, originally intended for a skirt. I decided to try to make a box with drawers, such that the drawer fronts would not be detectable if I were able to match the stripes carefully. Another of my many hobbies is calligraphy and the design of this box caters for the basic equipment required: A4 paper and quills, rulers, etc. in the deep slots at the back; nib holders and pencils in the trays on the top; bottles of ink in the deep bottom drawer and nibs, erasers, paper tissues and so on in the two small drawers.

Keepsakes box

This was created for a Cheshire Federation of Women's Institutes (FWI) competition at the County Show and was subsequently entered in the Shropshire FWI competition at the West Midlands Show and at Bingley Hall in Staffordshire – it came second in all three. The theme for the Cheshire Show was 'Take Time' and the logo was an egg timer, so the drawer pulls are watchface buttons and the logo is depicted in goldwork on each side, with the word 'Keepsakes' in gold lettering on the lid.

The outer fabric is silk. I started by making the two small drawers and casings at the front, then the long casing and drawer to match these measurements. I then added four casings and drawers (two on each side) behind. Next, I cut the side, front and back panels and lined the upper layer with a shot brocade to tone with the silk outer fabric. Finally, I hinged the lid and mounted the whole box on a platform base.

Advent box

Another box created for a Cheshire FWI competition, this time for 'an Advent Calendar using any craft medium': I think I won because mine was the only box.

It look a long time to design and construct (the schedule was published in November and I only finished it a few days before the Show the following June) and involved cutting 192 pieces of card. 'Advent' is written on the lid in uncial letters cut from gold kid, padded and stitched, with a gold thread couched around. Red, green, blue, yellow and purple silk are used inside the box, all colours which appear in the paisley design of the outer fabric. There is a pull-out platform for the Nativity Scene, which gradually evolves as the animal figures are removed from the 24 tiny boxes on the top layer; as the appropriate numbered box is opened each day and the contents placed on the platform, the red or green lid is turned over to reveal a blue or yellow lining when it is replaced on its box. On Christmas Day, the lids form a gold cross with a blue surround. The 'stained glass windows' inside the main lid are embroidered using the colour through gold technique.

RESOURCES

Mail-order suppliers

Needles

I have found it extremely difficult to obtain small curved needles – so essential to the maker of fabric-covered boxes – from the local haberdashery. However, a fine, curved, half round No. 12 needle (ref: 12 FNHR) is obtainable from the following mail-order supplier:

Forge Mill Needle Museum
Needle Mill Lane
Riverside
Redditch
Worcs B97 6RR
Tel: 01527 62509

Fabrics

Georgeous fabrics are now widely available through many outlets. The following supplier offers a wide variety of cottons, plain and decorated, by mail order.

The Cotton Patch
1285 Stratford Road
Hall Green
Birmingham B28 9AJ
Tel: 0121 702 2840
Freephone UK orders: 0800 0560509
Fax: 0121 778 5924
E-mail: jgsewel@ibm.net

Card

The 2mm ($\frac{3}{32}$in) thick card used for making boxes is generally available from art/craft shops or from local picture framers, who probably use it as a backing medium. However, in the event of difficulty in obtaining such card, supplies can be obtained by mail order from:

Craft Creations Ltd
Units 1–7
Harpers Yard
Ruskin Road
Tottenham
London N17 8QA
Tel: 0181 885 2655
Fax: 0181 808 0746

Kits of cut card for boxes

Jackie Woolsey
The Firs
Dicks Mount
Burgh St Peter
Beccles NR34 OBU
Tel: 01502 677304
E-mail: jackiewoolsey@talk21.com

On my bookshelf

Decorative Boxes, Bawden, Juliet
Charles Letts, London, 1993
ISBN 1 85238 416 6

Making Decorative Fabric-Covered Boxes,
Hiney, Mary Jo, Sterling, New York, 1996
ISBN 0 8069 1296 0

Embroidered Boxes, Lemon, Jane
Batsford, London, 1984
ISBN 0 7134 4587 4

The Cartonnage Kit, Luke, Heather
Little, Brown, London, 1995
ISBN 0 316 91390 1

Beautiful Boxes, Newman, Judy
Sally Milner, Australia, 1990
ISBN 1 86351 008 7

Boxes, Robinson, Debby
Anaya Publishers (imprint of
Collins & Brown), London, 1994
ISBN 1 85470 225 4

Index

About the author

Jackie is a qualified Crafts Judge, Demonstrator and Travelling Tutor for the National Federation of Women's Institutes (NFWI) and is President of the South Cheshire Branch of the Embroiderers' Guild. Although arriving somewhat unexpectedly in the world of crafts as the result of moving to the country after a professional career, Jackie has taught fabric-covered box making for many years in Adult Education, and tutored courses for Embroiderers' Guilds, Women's Institutes and Townswomen's Guilds, as well as at the NFWI's Denman College. She has also contributed articles on the subject to national magazines.

Jackie is the author of *Calligraphy for Beginners* (WI Books) and has collaborated with Daphne J. Ashby to produce *Ribbon Embroidery* (David & Charles) and *Creative Embroidery Techniques using Colour through Gold* (Guild of Master Craftsman Publications). They have also written and published a booklet, *Why not make a Beaded Amulet Purse?*

Toymaking

Dolls' Houses & Miniatures

Crafts

The Home & Gardening

VIDEOS

MAGAZINES

Woodturning • Woodcarving • Furniture & Cabinetmaking • The Dolls' House Magazine
The Router • The ScrollSaw • Creative Crafts for the Home • BusinessMatters • Water Gardening

The above represents a full list of all titles currently published or scheduled to be published.
All are available direct from the Publishers or through bookshops, newsagents and specialist retailers.
To place an order, or to obtain a complete catalogue, contact:

GMC Publications

Castle Place, 166 High Street, Lewes, East Sussex BN7 1XU, United Kingdom Tel: 01273 488005 Fax: 01273 478606

Orders by credit card are accepted